THE MESSAGE
WE
PROCLAIM

Gordon Clinard

Convention Press

NASHVILLE   TENNESSEE

© 1966 • CONVENTION PRESS

NASHVILLE, TENNESSEE

All rights reserved
International copyright secured.

5107-08

Code Number: Church Study Course
This book is number 0708 in category 7
section for Adults

Library of Congress Catalog Card Number: 66-10253
Printed in the United States of America
60. AT 65 R.R.D.

ABOUT THE AUTHOR

H. GORDON CLINARD was born in Springfield, Tennessee, April 14, 1922. He received his college education at Union University, Jackson, Tennessee, where he graduated with the A.B. degree in 1944. He attended Southwestern Baptist Theological Seminary, Fort Worth, Texas, where he received the B.D. and Th.D. degrees. Since 1955, he has been professor of preaching at Southwestern Seminary.

Prior to his seminary professorship, Dr. Clinard was pastor of churches in Tennessee and Texas. His last pastorate was the First Baptist Church, Huntsville, Texas. He has served numerous churches as interim pastor, including the First Baptist Church, Paris, Texas; Emmanuel Baptist Church, Alexandria, Louisiana; First Baptist Church, Wichita, Kansas; First Baptist Church, Altus, Oklahoma; First Baptist Church, Ponca City, Oklahoma; Beech Street Baptist Church, Texarkana, Arkansas; and First Baptist Church of St. Johns, St. Louis, Missouri. In addition, he has been used widely as a revival, Convention, assembly, and conference preacher.

Dr. Clinard is the coauthor of *Steps to the Sermon* and has contributed to numerous Baptist periodicals and sermon collections. He is the past editor of the *Southwestern Journal of Theology*.

Dr. Clinard and his wife, Christine, have two children, Patricia and Truitt.

PREFACE

In 1963, the Sunday School Board of the Southern Baptist Convention commissioned a committee to write a study paper for use in the Convention's 1965–66 emphasis on Proclamation and Witness. The committee was headed by H. C. Brown, professor of preaching, Southwestern Baptist Theological Seminary, and was composed of several Baptist pastors, members of Southwestern's faculty, denominational leaders, and laymen from the Fort Worth-Dallas area. It was my privilege to serve as the writer for the committee.

Many of the ideas for this book were born in the numerous discussions and written work of the committee. I am indebted to these men for their large share in this study.

My colleagues on the faculty of Southwestern encouraged me in the work on the book. Dr. H. C. Brown read the manuscript and made many valuable suggestions. My secretaries, Miss Joyce Bray and Mrs. Bob Poinsett, worked diligently in typing the material. Miss Nannie Don Beaty demonstrated unusual concern and care in the final typing. My appreciation also is extended to I. Lamar Maffett and others at the Sunday School Board who offered encouragement and helpful suggestions for the writing.

H. Gordon Clinard

CONTENTS

CHURCH STUDY COURSE

THE CHURCH STUDY COURSE began October 1, 1959. It is a merger of three courses previously promoted by the Sunday School Board —the Sunday School Training Course, the Graded Training Union Study Course, and the Church Music Training Course. On October 1, 1961, the Woman's Missionary Union principles and methods studies were added.

The course is fully graded. The system of awards provides a series of five diplomas of twenty books each for adults or Young People, two diplomas of five books each for Intermediates, and two diplomas of five books each for Juniors.

The course is comprehensive, with books grouped into twenty categories. The purpose of the course is to help Christians to grow in knowledge and conviction, to help them to grow toward maturity in Christian character and competence for service, to encourage them to participate worthily as workers in their churches, and to develop leaders for all phases of church life and work.

The Church Study Course is promoted by the Baptist Sunday School Board, 127 Ninth Avenue, North, Nashville, Tennessee, through its Sunday School, Training Union, Church Music, and Church Administration departments; and the Woman's Missionary Union, 600 North Twentieth Street, Birmingham, Alabama; and by the respective departments in the states affiliated with the Southern Baptist Convention. A description of the course and the system of awards may be found in the leaflet "Trained Workmen," which may be obtained without charge from any one of these departments named.

A record of all awards earned should be maintained in each church. A person should be designated by the church to keep the files. Forms for such records may be ordered from any Baptist Book Store.

REQUIREMENTS FOR CREDIT IN CLASS
OR HOME STUDY

IF CREDIT is desired for the study of this book in a class or by home study, the following requirements must be met:

I. IN CLASSWORK

1. The class must meet a minimum of seven and one-half clock hours. The required times does not include assembly periods. Ten class periods of forty-five minutes each are recommended. (If laboratory or clinical work is desired in specialized or technical courses, this requirement may be met by six clock hours of classwork and three clock hours of supervised laboratory or clinical work.)

2. A class member who attends all class sessions and completes the reading of the book within a week following the last class session will not be required to do any written work.

3. A class member who is absent from one or more sessions must answer the questions on all chapters he misses. In such a case, he must turn in his paper within a week, and he must certify that he has read the book.

4. The teacher should request an award for himself. A person who teaches a book in the section for Intermediates or Juniors of any category or conducts an approved unit of instruction for Nursery, Beginner, or Primary children will be granted an award in category 11, Special Studies, which will count as an elective on his own diploma. He should specify in his request the name of the book taught, or the unit conducted for Nursery, Beginner, or Primary children.

5. The teacher should complete the "Request for Book Awards —Class Study" (Form 150) and forward it within two weeks after the completion of the class to the Church Study Course Awards Office, 127 Ninth Avenue, North, Nashville, Tennessee 37203.

II. IN HOME STUDY

1. A person who does not attend any class session may receive credit by answering all questions for written work as indicated

in the book. When a person turns in his paper on home study, he must certify that he has read the book.

2. Students may find profit in studying the text together, but individual papers are required. Carbon copies or duplicates in any form cannot be accepted.

3. Home study work papers may be graded by the pastor or a person designated by him or they may be sent to the Church Study Course Awards Office for grading. The form entitled "Request for Book Awards—Home Study" (Form 151) must be used in requesting awards. It should be mailed to Church Study Course Awards Office, 127 Ninth Avenue, North, Nashville, Tennessee 37203.

III. CREDIT FOR THIS BOOK

This book is number 0708 in category 7, section for Adults.

The Message We Proclaim

CHAPTER 1

1

Proclamation—
The Christian Mission

CHRISTIAN PROCLAMATION means giving witness to God's redemptive act in Christ. It addresses the non-Christian world primarily, but it also includes informing and inspiring the Christian that he may grow "to the measure of the stature of the fulness of Christ" (Eph. 4:13, RSV). Effective proclamation depends on the work of the Holy Spirit, through whose witness Christ himself becomes the proclaimer. The public preaching of judgment and grace is essential to the declaration of the gospel, but the means of this proclamation are many.

The proclamation of God's grace in Christ is central to the Christian experience(It is the mission of the church and an inescapable demand upon every Christian) This centrality indicates the importance of proclamation and explains the aims of this study. It is our objective to gain a better understanding of the purpose and content of proclamation as the Christian mission. Thus, may we challenge every Christian to recognize and participate in his opportunities to proclaim the gospel.

I. THE NEED TO UNDERSTAND PROCLAMATION

Evidence abounds that a study of proclamation is needed. Consider, for example, the failure of many Christians to participate in, or to fully understand the theology of, the Christian witness. Let us consider some of these evidences before proceeding with the study.

1. *The Need for a New Understanding of Preaching*

Christian history attests that the greatest advances of the gospel have been made during times of great preaching. Though able men have lived and preached in every century, the first, fourth, thirteenth, sixteenth, and nineteenth centuries have been the periods when preaching reached its highest status. Each of these centuries was marked by significant Christian reform and advance. It is true for all of Christianity, and especially of Baptists, that much progress will not be made beyond the strength of the pulpit.

What is the quality of preaching in our century? Although the matter can be vigorously debated, it is likely true that preaching has declined during the first half of the twentieth century. A large reason for this decline has been that ministers and congregations alike have been uncertain as to the theology of preaching as proclamation.

The question, Who is the preacher? cries out for an answer. Tensions eat away at the minister's sense of identity. He struggles to be a person, but he is pressured to fulfil a ministerial image forced upon him. He wants to speak prophetically for God, but he also wants to be a popular pulpiteer. Resistance to prophetic preaching on controversial issues is all too common. Fulfilling the biblical image of the minister as servant runs against the "Madison Avenue" demand that he produce in statistical and material achievements. His conviction that preaching is his primary task loses its sharpness against the dulling fatigue that accompanies his many labors. He is administrator, community leader, teacher, counselor, financier, and promoter. Where is the time for preparing to preach? The image of the minister is confused. Just who is he anyway?

Preaching suffers more seriously from an inadequate concept of the content of true proclamation. Much that is called preaching does not qualify as such biblically and theologically. Many sermons are relevant to their times, but, because they are lacking in biblical content, they do not convey biblical authority. Other preaching uses biblical terms without participating in the dynamic qualities of biblical revelation or the intent of the biblical message. This preaching is neither relevant nor biblical. Such preaching can be compared to a telephone that provides only long distance service. In order to be both biblical and relevant, the preacher must proclaim the Word of God to current expressions of man's universal and unchanging spiritual needs.

More than the minister, the evidence testifies, congregations need to understand preaching as proclamation. Since church members are also vital to preaching, H. H. Farmer is correct in that all within that Christian community ought to understand clearly and deeply *what is supposed to be happening when preaching is taking place and solemnly acknowledge their responsibility in and for it.*[1] Such an understanding will enhance the congregation's belief in the priority of preaching for Christian proclamation. It also will clarify their image of the ministry, deepen their participation in worship, and help to guarantee the freedom of the pulpit. One of the main purposes of this study will be to improve preaching through a better understanding of proclamation.

2. *The Need for Personal Involvement in Witnessing*

Recently, a member of a large Baptist church lamented, "Out of the six hundred we have in Sunday school and church on Sunday morning, we are fortunate to have thirty who show up for visitation during the week." Personal witnessing is not limited to an organized visitation program. Yet the

---

[1] *The Servant of the Word* (Philadelphia: Fortress Press, 1942), p. viii.

church member's statement emphasizes a major weakness in our churches. That is the meager involvement of church members in Christian witness. A major factor in this problem is their failure to understand the purpose and nature of proclamation.

Many Baptists think of themselves as supporters of their pastor, who is to do the work of proclamation. They have never grasped the full meaning of the priesthood of the believer. They fail to recognize that preaching also can, and must, be done through their personal testimony. They do not understand that every Christian is called to a ministry of witnessing. Unfortunately, many Christians lack a sense of urgency and concern for the unsaved. Many others, feeling an awareness of their involvement in proclamation, hesitate to bear personal witness because they lack training.

The most effective outreach of our churches awaits an understanding that all who know Christ are involved in his redemptive purposes and, hence, must proclaim him to mankind. Certainly, one of the results of the Southern Baptist emphasis on proclamation should be the enlistment and training of Christians in personal witnessing.

3. *The Need for Effective Proclamation by Christian Living*

The Christian probably bears his most effective witness to Christ through his character and personal relationships. Church membership does not mean a great deal for many. The idea that the Christian community is a company of the committed makes little impact upon large segments of any church's members. Many who call themselves Christian make all of life's decisions and value judgments upon the same bases as do those in the world. What men appear to be within the church fellowship does not always make a difference in their lives beyond the church. Some apparently have attempted to accept Christ as Saviour from sin without claiming him as Lord of life. This violates the New Testament's description of discipleship (Matt. 16:24; Mark 10:17–21). And it robs the Christian and the church of their power to influence the world.

A study of proclamation should result in the deepening of Christian commitment and a greater insistence upon a redeemed church membership. More Christians should come to realize that Christian living proclaims Christ eloquently.

4. *The Need for New Penetrations of the World*

The Christian dialogue with the world demands creative attention in our time. Our increasing desertion of the inner city and an accompanying failure to penetrate the changing cosmopolitan culture leave a great void in the proclamation of the gospel. The population explosion and the rapidly changing world situation compel the examination of new mission and communication methods. New efforts must be made to communicate with vast segments of our culture. These segments were once highly influenced by Christianity but, now, are amazingly divorced from an effective dialogue with our churches. Such areas as the arts and higher education illustrate these cultural segments. What can help more to reestablish contacts than a new understanding of the nature and means of Christian proclamation?

5. *Other Needs*

The evidence for the worth of a study of proclamation and witness is greater yet. The need to strengthen our theology of worship pertains to our study also. The concept of proclamation as central to worship must be matched by an understanding of worship as proclamation. Not only must we listen for God's voice in the sermon. A recognition of proclamation in the hymns, in the reading of the Scripture passages, in baptism, and in the Lord's Supper will make worship more meaningful. We need to understand that the entire congregation preaches to the world in its public worship. This understanding will transform the experience for the worshiper from spectator to participant. This study of proclamation, then, should deepen the Christian's sense of worship, public and private.

Again, the large numbers in our churches who are untrained in biblical knowledge and in Christian doctrine and those who are unstable in the storms which characterize the human experience demand effective proclamation. A broader interpretation of Christian witness and evangelism obviously would be redemptive. The gospel must be announced to men but, once announced and accepted, it must also be applied and taught. The new Christian must be instructed, inspired, and strengthened.

The mention of these areas of need will show the importance of our study. The fullest motivation for pursuing the subject further, however, depends upon an understanding that proclamation is demanded by the nature of Christianity. In short, we need a theology *for* proclamation before we shall be willing to search for a theology *of* proclamation.

II. THE DEMAND FOR PROCLAMATION

Proclamation and the Christian gospel are corollaries. New Testament scholars emphasize this when they insist that to think of Christianity is to think of preaching. At least four theological demands for Christian proclamation exist.

1. *The Nature of God and His Revelation*

The basis of all proclamation is the self-disclosure of a personal God. God has chosen to reveal himself to man. Otherwise, man could never have known him. We understand this more readily when we recall that it is of the essence of selfhood that a person must *will* to be known; he must give himself to others, if he will be known at all. Therefore, man never discovers God. The initiative in revelation belongs to God.

No Christian, upon careful analysis, feels that he "found God." Rather, he knows that God found him, loved him, and redeemed him.

God primarily revealed himself in his mighty acts. Paul writes that God's acts in nature are revelatory. "For since the creation of the world His invisible attributes, His eternal power and divine nature, have been clearly seen, being understood through what has been made, so that they are without excuse" (Rom. 1:20, NASB[2]). In such events as creation itself, the deliverance of a chosen nation, and his redemptive intervention in that nation's destiny, God acted in history to disclose himself.

God also revealed himself in what he said through his prophets. Revelation, however, was climaxed, in the sense of a complete and final self-disclosure, in Jesus: "When in former times God spoke to our forefathers, he spoke in fragmentary and varied fashion through the prophets. But in this the final age he has spoken to us in the Son whom he has made heir to the whole universe, and through whom he created all orders of existence: the Son who is the effulgence of God's splendour and the stamp of God's very being, and sustains the universe by his word of power" (Heb. 1:1–3, NEB[3]).

In his redemptive deed in Christ, God laid himself bare to man. Here was the unique and final giving of himself. "And the Word became flesh, and dwelt among us, we beheld His glory, glory as of the Only Begotten from the Father" (John 1:14, NASB). The question, What is God like? has been eternally and finally answered. He is, and has always been, like Jesus, for "No man has seen God at any time; the only begotten God, who is in the bosom of the Father, He has ex-

---

[2] *New American Standard Bible, New Testament,* © The Lockman Foundation, 1960, 1962, 1963.

[3] © the Delegates of the Oxford University Press and the Syndics of the Cambridge University Press, 1961.

plained Him" (John 1:18, NASB). Jesus has allowed man to see and to know God.

God so disclosed himself in Jesus because it is his heart to search for man. From the cry to Adam, "Where art thou?" (Gen. 3:9, ASV) to the word of the angel to the puzzled Joseph, "You shall give him the name Jesus (Saviour), for he will save his people from their sins" (Matt. 1:21, NEB), to the Holy Spirit's tug at the will of man today, God has been in search for man. That search was climaxed in his redemptive move into history in Jesus.

Proclamation occurs in the faith that God, who has so revealed himself redemptively, continuously reveals himself to man. We must proclaim the good news, not because it is our nature to do so primarily, but because it is God's nature to reveal himself to man. Indeed, proclamation is God's continuing pursuit of his sovereign purpose to disclose himself and to redeem man from his sin.

2. *The Nature of Man and His Predicament*

The redemptive mission of Christ implies the human predicament (Mark 1:4; Luke 1:76–77; 19:10). Man is a sinner. Every man has sinned. Paul wrote, "For there is no distinction; for all have sinned, and fall short of the glory of God" (Rom. 3:22–23, ASV). He did not mean that all men have sinned equally, but that all, without exception, have sinned. P. T. Forsyth well described the human predicament when he said: "What we have with each soul is rather a fresh case than a new development." [4]

The biblical language portrays the nature of man's sin vividly. Psalm 51, for example, contains three of the most descriptive terms used in the Old Testament to explain man's depravity. Sin is transgression (v. 1), a deliberate rebellion

———————

[4] *Positive Preaching and the Modern Mind* (Grand Rapids: Wm. B. Eerdmans Publishing Co., 1964), p. 36.

against God. Sin is iniquity (v. 2), moral crookedness, a perverse turning from the straight and righteous. Sin is "missing the mark" (v. 2), a failure to measure up, a wandering from the way. The New Testament describes man's sin in terms of wickedness (Heb. 8:12), responsible transgression (Rom. 5:12), unfaithfulness (Heb. 3:12), maliciousness (I Cor. 5:8), lawlessness (Rom. 6:19), evil desire (James 1:14), and in other equally realistic language. The Genesis account of original sin accurately reveals man's rebellious act—sin is man's proud refusal to be a creature of God. It is his effort to be his own god. It is revolt, mutiny against God and the person God made man to be. And this rebellion involves man's total being. As Frank Stagg suggests, the Bible would have us know that man "is in trouble in his thinking, in his emotional responses, in his volitional choices, in his moral values, in his bodily expression, in his relationship to God, to other people, and to things." [5]

The result of man's sin is alienation from God (Eph. 4:18). The gulf between man and God is far more than the separation of Creator and creature. Man's sin breaks his communion with God. It puts him at enmity with God. Therefore, the result of sin is death (Rom. 6:23; Eph. 2:1). Man needs, not an example, but a Saviour. He needs redemption, not reform. He needs new life, not new goals. The barrier which he has built between himself and God must be removed, and only God can remove it. Man must have new life. He must be spiritually renewed, and only God can cause such a new beginning.

God's grace has moved to redeem man from his hopeless condition. The plight of man moved upon God's heart. The same plight demands proclamation of the good news of redemption in our time.

---

[5] *New Testament Theology* (Nashville: Broadman Press, 1962), p. 32.

3. The Nature of the Christian Experience

The very nature of the Christian experience and life demands proclamation of the gospel. The new life which the believer receives in salvation is the life of God himself. Paul frequently wrote of the Christian as "in Christ" and surely meant that the Christian participates in the life of Christ. When we commit our lives to Christ, we are inevitably caught up in his redemptive mission in the world. The Christian has no choice. The same redemptive act which gave him new life now compels him to proclaim Christ. And so it is in the Christian community. Those who have seen the glory of God must bear witness of that glory. In all reality, then, the nonwitnessing Christian and the nonwitnessing church are impossibilities.

Aside from the nature of the Christian experience, the believer's commitment to the lordship of Christ makes proclamation inevitable. For the commands of Christ to witness are explicit. The people of God can scarcely ignore the imperatives of Matthew 28:19–20; John 20:21; and Acts 1:8. Jesus, assuming that his disciples would go, said, "Make disciples . . . baptizing . . . teaching." He committed his ministry to his followers, "As my Father hath sent me, even so send I you." As his disciples stood on the threshold of their great venture, the resurrected Christ commissioned them, "Ye shall be witnesses unto me both in Jerusalem, and in all Judaea, and Samaria, and unto the uttermost part of the earth." Proclamation thus becomes the Christian's inevitable mission.

4. The Nature of the Gospel

Many theologians speak of the gospel as a proclaimed gospel. They mean that the nature of the gospel is such that it must be proclaimed. Indeed, as we shall later observe in our discussion of the theology of proclamation, they mean that witness is a part of the gospel. Much truth resides in the concept. To understand it is to be compelled further to proclamation.

Man has been created of God as personal, wilful, and free. Because both God and man are personal, revelation of necessity is personal. God revealed himself in a person, Jesus Christ. Redemption is a personal meeting with Christ. Such a gospel demands proclamation, for God will not violate man's freedom by coercion. Rather, he entreats man. God speaks to man, but he does not force him. Man is left free to hear and to accept God's redemptive love for himself. Because of the personal nature of redemption, God has never been without his witnesses who plead for their fellows to hear and obey God. Such was the intended witness of the covenant people, Israel. Such is the actual mission of the Christian community.

But the gospel also concerns a <u>deed</u>. Revelation is a <u>deed of God</u> in history. God has acted in Christ to redeem men. Thus, the gospel demands proclamation because it is the <u>nature of an event to be told.</u> The gospel is good news. This fact may be clarified by an illustration. Suppose that, by a mighty act of deliverance, all of the enslaved peoples of the world were made free. Suppose that someone was sent to them who was so anxious they learn of their deliverance that he would tell them the news. It would be of the nature of the news that it must be told. In fact, it would not be news for those enslaved until it was told. So it is the essence of the gospel of man's deliverance in Christ that the gospel be proclaimed to those enslaved by their sin.

This chapter has sought to underscore the need for proclamation and the desire to proclaim. The need to understand and to become involved in proclamation can be seen partially in our <u>inadequate concepts</u> of (1) preaching, (2) personal witnessing, (3) the witness of the Christian life, (4) the Christian penetration of the world, (5) worship, and (6) Christian nurture and education. The demand for proclamation has been seen to reside in (1) the nature of God's revelation, (2) the predicament and freedom of man, (3) the nature of Christian discipleship, and (4) the nature of the gospel itself. In the opening sentences of the chapter, a definition of proclamation was given. If we are to understand the task of proclamation, we must now test that definition by the Bible.

FOR STUDY AND CLASS DISCUSSION

FOR FURTHER STUDY

1. This chapter has made the claim that the periods of greatest Christian advance have been the periods of powerful preaching. You may wish to read more about the history of Christian preaching. The volumes by Edwin C. Dargan, *A History of Preaching* (Grand Rapids: Baker Book House, 1954) and John A. Broadus, *Lectures on the History of Preaching* (New York: A. C. Armstrong and Son, 1901) are classics in this field. Your church library may have one or both of these volumes.

2. It would be helpful to read Findley B. Edge, *A Quest for Vitality in Religion* (Nashville: Broadman Press, 1963) and Elton Trueblood, *The Company of the Committed* (New York: Harper and Bros., 1961) for a further study of the command that every Christian must witness to the gospel.

FOR DISCUSSION AND CLASSWORK

1. List on page 15 some of the problems about witnessing with which you are familiar.

2. How has your Christian experience led you to believe that the gospel must be proclaimed?

3. Describe some things about the problems of modern man that make the proclamation of the gospel necessary in our time.

Some Problems Concerning Witnessing

1. No double standards for

2.

3.

4.

5.

CHAPTER 2

I. THE OLD TESTAMENT—PREPARATION FOR PROCLAMATION
   1. A Primary Emphasis on Exhortation
   2. Witness Beyond the Covenant
   3. Stage for New Testament Proclamation set in Old Testament

II. THE NEW TESTAMENT—THE ACT AND CONTENT OF CHRISTIAN PROCLAMATION
   1. The Act of Witnessing
   2. The Content of Christian Proclamation

III. THE PROBLEM—IS PROCLAMATION LIMITED TO A GOSPEL WITNESS TO UNBELIEVERS?

2

Proclamation—
A Biblical Theology

HOW DOES THE OLD TESTAMENT contribute to an understanding of Christian proclamation? What does a study of the proclamation of Jesus and the apostles teach us about the act and content of Christian witness in our time? Is proclamation limited to witness to the unsaved, as some scholars such as C. H. Dodd would have us believe? These questions will guide us as we seek a biblical theology of proclamation.

I. THE OLD TESTAMENT—PREPARATION FOR PROCLAMATION

Christian proclamation means witness to the "good tidings" of the gospel. The Old Testament, then, contains preparation for Christian proclamation, rather than proclamation itself. Let us see what this involves.

1. A *Primary Emphasis on Exhortation*

Almost always, the vocal presentation of God's message in the Old Testament is exhortation addressed to those in covenant relation with Jehovah. Several words suggesting a proclamation occur. When they do not refer to some general declaration by rulers, however, they usually describe divine or prophetic announcement of an epochal event to the nation. One such word means "to cause a voice to pass over"

17

or "to announce." Nehemiah 8:15 illustrates its common usage, a public announcement or proclamation of a significant event to God's people.

The predominant Old Testament term translated "to proclaim" literally means "to call." With one exception, noted later, every use of the term refers either to proclamation within the covenant relationship or to some nonreligious declaration. God proclaimed his name to Moses (Ex. 33:19; 34:5–6); Jeremiah proclaimed judgment and called to repentance (Jer. 3:12; 7:2; 19:2); rulers called for fasts and the public recognition of some person of esteem, or they issued edicts of various kinds (Jonah 3:5; Jer. 34:8; 1 Kings 21:9).

Covenant usage continued in most of the other Old Testament words having to do with proclamation. Ecclesiastes refers to "the preacher" by using the term "caller." But it hints at nothing approximating the Christian witness to the world. Only one usage of the verb "to bring good tidings" or "to preach" indicates anything other than exhortation within the redeemed community.

A careful examination of prophecy also confirms the predominance of exhortation in the Old Testament. The prophets primarily spoke the word of a moral God in application to religious experience, the existing religious institution, and public life. They warned, encouraged, cried out against the social and political evils of their day, and thrillingly raised the hope of the people for an indescribably future glory. But the prophet, in it all, remained primarily a chosen man "forth-telling" God's message to a chosen people. The principal thrust of the Old Testament witness is exhortation, rather than "gospel preaching."

2. *Witness Beyond the Covenant*

There are, however, exceptions to the conclusion above. These more closely approximate the understanding of Christian proclamation. Two Old Testament passages are clearly evangelistic. Jonah 3:2 records that God commanded the prophet to "go unto Nineveh, that great city, and preach unto it the preaching that I bid thee" (ASV). Jonah's mission was evangelistic, for he was to preach to the Gentiles. Two words for proclaim, "to call" and "to preach" or "to bring good tidings," are used in Isaiah's announcement of coming salvation: "The Spirit of the Lord God is upon me; because the Lord hath anointed me to preach good tidings unto the meek; he hath sent me to bind up the brokenhearted, to proclaim liberty to the captives, and the opening of the prison to them that are bound; to proclaim the acceptable year of the Lord" (Isa. 61:1–2). Jesus' use of the Isaiah passage to inaugurate his ministry (Luke 4:16–21) proves it to be both eschatological and evangelistic in nature.

In addition to the Jonah and Isaiah passages, two New Testament references reflect an Old Testament use of proclamation as redemptive outreach. Jude 14 states that Enoch prophesied. Both the word used, a term sometimes rendered "to preach," and the content of the prophecy indicate an evangelistic concern. Noah is described as a "preacher of righteousness" in 2 Peter 2:5. The noun used is "herald." This term is used in the New Testament to describe one who heralds the gospel message to the world. Some scholars find evangelistic overtones reflected in Joel 3:9 and Isaiah 62:11. The best scholars, however, usually hold that Jonah 3:2, Isaiah 62:1–2, Jude 14, and 2 Peter 2:5 are the only clear references to redemptive witness beyond the covenant in the Old Testament.

The Jonah passage reminds us of Israel's mission to bear a redemptive relation to the world. This is an important facet of proclamation in the Old Testament. God made that mission clear in his call to Abram: "And I will make of thee a great nation, and I will bless thee, and make thy name great; and be thou a blessing" (Gen. 12:2, ASV). The nation, through her exclusiveness, failed to fulfil her mission and was thus dispossessed of her redemptive opportunity. Yet, individuals within the nation had a growing consciousness of Israel's intended worldwide destiny. It is true that the prophets spoke primarily to those within the covenant, but they did so in an effort to help them to fulfil the nation's purpose in salvation history. In this emphasis on the people of God as God's chosen instruments to bless a world, the Old Testament speaks with eloquent and solemn clarity to the Christian church.

Proclamation as evangelism may be implied elsewhere in the Old Testament. John A. Broadus calls the addresses of the patriarchs "ancient sermons." [1] Many of the prophets rose above the narrow nationalism of Israel. They dared to take the entire world in the name of the sovereign Jehovah and often called all the nations of the earth to judgment. Read Isaiah 10:5–19, 14–19; and Amos 1 to 2:3.

Some scholars have spoken of the prophets as more nearly possessing and proclaiming what we now call the gospel than has been supposed. However, Edwin C. Dargan reflects the best conclusion to be drawn from the Old Testament evidences: "Prophecy was preparation only." [2] So it was with Old Testament proclamation in general.

3. Stage for New Testament Proclamation Set in Old Testament

Preparation, as foundational, is essential. At least three important areas of the Christian witness are foreshadowed in the Old Testament.

(1) *Proclamation as God's outreach for man.*—God's election and deliverance of Israel clearly revealed his purpose to

---

[1] *Lectures on the History of Preaching* (New York: A. C. Armstrong and Son, 1901), pp. 5-10.

[2] *A History of Preaching* (New York: Hodder & Stoughton, George H. Doran Co., 1905), I, 21.

redeem man. We have noted that it is the Christian's inescapable responsibility to bear witness to his faith. And we have seen that this comes from the nature and initiative of God before it arises from the nature of man or the essence of the Christian's experience. The heart of God has not changed. It is not his desire that any should perish. God still searches for rebellious man. But his redemption of sinful humanity required a deed of redemption. His election of Israel as a chosen nation, through whom he could bless the world, was a primary act in the salvation history. This act was climaxed in Christ, and Christians are now involved in it as proclaimers of the gospel.

(2) *Old Testament terms for proclamation.*—The Old Testament words for proclamation are used almost always in a general context, or as exhortation addressed to Israel. However, these words cast light on the nature of the Christian witness. Such words include "to announce" or "to cause a voice to pass over" (Neh. 8:15), "to call" (Jer. 3:12), "to cause to hear" (Isa. 62:11), "a voice" (2 Chron. 24:9), "a loud cry" (1 Kings 22:36), "to cry as a herald" (Dan. 5:29), "to preach" or "to bring good tidings" (Psalm 40:9), "the preacher" (Eccl. 1:1–2), and "the preaching" (Jonah 3:2). These words have their New Testament counterparts. They give insight into the nature and means of a Christian's proclamation. They describe the urgency of the task of the performer. And this urgency later will be associated with the Christian witness.

(3) *The Old Testament prophets.*—The prophets are vital to the Old Testament's preparation for the preaching of the gospel. Some would discount the contemporary minister's spiritual lineage from the prophets. These persons insist that the prophets spoke from an immediate revelation impossible for the minister, who is only a steward of that revelation. The Christian preacher, however, in many respects descends from the Old Testament seers.

Consider, for example, the prophet's call. He spoke under the compulsion that God had placed him in the task that he pursued. Amos affirmed, "I was no prophet, neither was I a prophet's son; but I was an herdman, and a gatherer of sycomore fruit: and the Lord took me as I followed the flock, and the Lord said unto me, Go, prophesy unto my people Israel" (Amos 7:14–15).

Jeremiah was sure of his calling, for he had heard God say, "Before I formed thee in the belly I knew thee; and before thou camest forth out of the womb I sanctified thee, and I ordained thee a prophet unto the nations." (Jer. 1:5). Every Christian shares in the calling to minister. There remains, however, for the man whom we call "preacher" a unique call not unlike that which the prophet received.

The prophet was called to become a spokesman for God. He was literally to be a "forthteller." He was to bear the message of Another. This aspect of Old Testament proclamation needs to be recovered by pastors and congregations today. This recovery would give to ministers a new sense of stewardship about preaching and to congregations both a new respect for preaching and for the freedom of the preacher as God's spokesman.

The prophet spoke for God out of his deep personal relationship with God. Thus, his message rang with the authority of revelation. His proclamation was filled with such references as, "The word of the Lord that came unto" (Hosea 1:1), "Then said the Lord unto me" (Hosea 3:1), "Therefore saith the Lord" (Isa. 1:24). "Thus saith the Lord" added urgency to the prophet's manner and authority to his utterances. The origin of his message explains his devotion to it, regardless of the popular response. His function was to speak for God without respect to the nature of his response. He did not speak to please men with words that they liked to hear. He spoke to fulfil his function as God's mouthpiece.

And because he spoke for God, the prophet spoke to the

people about the specific needs of his own time. He represented a moral God. Thus, he did not hesitate to speak of the personal, religious, political, and social sins of his people. Yet, he was no social reformer as such. It was his devotion to the redemptive purposes of a moral God that prompted his ethical sermons. Ethics and theology were united in the prophets. The noted Old Testament teacher Otto J. Baab writes, "The prophet selects his themes, formulates his ideas, and delivers his sermon on the basis of his passionate commitment to the covenant God of justice and mercy." [3]

Since the prophet's message proceeded from God, it contained a sure word of hope. He believed in a God who is redemptively at work in history. He promised that out of God's judgment a purified and holy remnant of Israel would prevail (Isa. 10:21–22). He spoke of comfort as well as judgment (Isa. 40:1–2). He described a day of salvation as well as a day of accounting (Isa. 28:5–6). Prophets such as Isaiah, Micah, and Jeremiah spoke unmistakably of a messianic hope. Ezekiel assured his people of God's pleasure to save (Ezek. 33:11). Jeremiah promised a new covenant (Jer. 31:31–34). The prophets spoke for a God of mercy and power. They believed in his ultimate triumph. The implications of the prophetic message for Christian proclamation are clear.

In summary, the Old Testament gives rare insight into evangelistic proclamation. Its greatest contribution comes in its more common emphasis on exhortation to a covenant people. But God's effort to use his people redemptively, the Old Testament terms for exhortation, and the influence of the prophets upon the contemporary preacher—all are clearly preparatory for a New Testament understanding of proclamation and witness.

---

[3] *Prophetic Preaching a New Approach* (New York: Abingdon Press, 1948), p. 107.

II. THE NEW TESTAMENT—THE ACT AND CONTENT OF CHRISTAN PROCLAMATION

Several words in the New Testament describe the act and content of the oral communication of the gospel. The use of these different terms assures us that witnessing is no narrow concept in New Testament thought. Preaching in the public worship service, though central to the meaning of Christian witness, does not exhaust it.

1. *The Act of Witnessing*

Several words for the act of witnessing can be considered under three categories. They are words that deal with speaking to the world, and to unbelievers primarily. But some of these terms are used in a Christian context and to the Christian community.

(1) *Address to unbelievers.*—Two words are used consistently to refer to proclamation in the sense of witness to the unsaved. One of these words means "to proclaim as a herald." Translations usually render it "herald" or "preach," and more rarely "publish" or "proclaim." The word pictures a chosen herald of a king riding through the realm proclaiming whatever message the sovereign has decreed. Used for the Christian herald, it means the proclamation of the gospel. It is rendered "preach" in Matthew 4:17, Mark 16:15, Luke 9:2, Acts 8:5, Philippians 1:15, and in at least fifty other passages in the New Testament. It inevitably refers to proclamation to the world in an evangelistic sense, not to believers within the Christian community.

The other word for proclaiming the gospel to unbelievers means "to tell good news." The term most frequently used for preaching occurs about seventy times in the New Testament. It describes the *nature* of the message of Christian proclamation, the good news of salvation, whereas the word discussed above meaning "to herald" shows the *manner* of proclamation, heralding. The second word appears in such passages as Matthew 11:5, Luke 4:43, Acts 5:42, 1 Corinthians 1:17, Galatians 1:8, and Ephesians 2:17, where it is translated "preach" or "preached." The appearance of this word in Acts 8:35 proves that preaching in the New Testament vocabulary is a much broader term than has been commonly accepted. Speaking of Philip's conversation with the Ethiopian eunuch, the verse reads, "Then Philip opened his mouth, and began at the same scripture and preached unto him Jesus." Evidently preaching, in the sense of telling good news, occurs in personal witnessing as well as in public proclamation. We do well to remember two things about these words "to herald" and "to proclaim" good news: (a) these are the New Testament's most frequent words for proclamation or preaching, and (b) they consistently refer to address to an unbelieving world.

(2) *Address to the world and the church.*—Other words occur less frequently in the New Testament to describe Christian preaching. John's Gospel uses a graphic term, "witness," which pictures proclamation as the giving of a testimony based on personal experience (John 15:27; 19:35; 21:24). The term also appears in Acts 23:11, 1 Corinthians 15:15, 1 John 1:2, and in many other passages. It represents the proclaimer as a witness standing before the people to whom he speaks. As before a judge, he stands to tell what he knows firsthand about the gospel. Paul describes the seriousness of proclamation in the use of "witness" in 1 Corinthians 15:15. He declares that he is a fraud if the resurrection is false, for he has spoken of the living Christ on the basis of personal encounter with him. One form of the word "witness" appears in such passages as Acts 8:5 to depict the urgency of preaching. When witness is used in this way, the word carries the idea of "charge" and implies forceful presentation.

A word meaning "to tell thoroughly" appears eighteen times in the writings of Paul and in Acts (Acts 13:5; 17:3;

1 Cor. 9:14; Col. 1:28). It speaks of authority in preaching. The idea of witnessing as "speaking face to face" appears in the word translated "speak" in Matthew 13:13, 23:1, Mark 4:33, John 8:12, and 1 Corinthians 3:1. Like "to tell thoroughly," it also suggests a quality of effective proclamation.

An interesting insight into New Testament proclamation occurs in the use of the word translated "dispute" in Acts 17:17 and 19:8–9. The early proclaimer apparently reasoned, argued, and perhaps even engaged in oral dialogue with his audience in some of his presentations of the gospel.

In contrast with the terms "to herald" and "to proclaim good news," these latter words do not always refer to an address to unbelievers. For example, "to speak face to face" in Matthew 23:1 refers both to Jesus' address to the multitude and to his disciples. In 1 Corinthians 3:1, it describes address to the church. "Dispute" or "reason" occurs in Acts 20:7 in the context of the Christian fellowship at Troas. The word "witness on the basis of personal testimony," or "testify," describes admonition to Christians in Ephesians 4:17. Indeed, when translated "charge"—as in 1 Timothy 5:21, 2 Timothy 2:14, and 4:1—the passage usually refers to an address of ethical instruction.

(3) *Address to the Christian community.*—Some words in the New Testament occur rather consistently to denote communication with the Christian community.

One such word is "to teach," meaning "to hold discourse for purposes of instruction." This term appears approximately one hundred times to describe the ministry of Jesus and the apostles. Typical passages are Matthew 4:23; 21:23, Mark 1:21; 6:6, Acts 11:26, Romans 2:21, and Colossians 3:16. Often, the word's usage indicates a clear distinction between the acts of teaching and preaching in the ministry of Jesus. "And Jesus went about all Galilee, *teaching* in their synagogues, and *preaching* the gospel of the kingdom" (Matt. 4:23, Italics mine). The same distinction occurs in Matthew

9:35 and 11:1. Doubtless, to teach, both in the ministry of Christ and in the witness of the apostles, primarily meant to instruct believers in doctrine and Christian living. This act is contrasted with sharing the gospel with unbelievers described in the terms "to herald" and "to proclaim good news." Such teaching was based, however, on the gospel content proclaimed to the world.

Other terms having to do with instruction of the believer, but of less importance to an understanding of proclamation, are to "instruct" (Gal. 6:6), to "reprove" or to "convict" (2 Tim. 4:2), and to "train" (Titus 2:12).

The idea of exhortation occurs frequently in the New Testament, usually in the context of supportive preaching to the believer. The prevalent word used for exhortation means "to call to one's side to help." From this word comes *Paraclete*, the term Jesus used to speak of the Holy Spirit as our comforter (John 14:16). Once in the Gospels (Luke 3:18) the word "to call to one's side" appears as a synonym for preaching, and here it refers to the proclamation of John. The Pauline epistles and Acts often use the term to refer to preaching. Frequently, the meaning is for the encouragement of new Christians. It was the work of Barnabas at Antioch to exhort, encourage, "them all, that with purpose of heart they would cleave unto the Lord" (Acts 11:23). Paul used the same word to describe the mission of Timothy at Thessalonica: "to comfort you concerning your faith" (1 Thess. 3:2). Again, "exhort" sometimes carries the idea of an ethical urging. Such usage appears in 1 Timothy 6:2 and Titus 2:6.

These and many other words present a three-fold purpose in the presentation of the gospel—to evangelize, to teach, and to strengthen the Christian life. Three phrases emerge as of major importance to a biblical theology of proclamation: (*a*) to herald, (*b*) to proclaim the good news, and (*c*) to teach. These phrases raise a problem for the definition of proclamation. See subhead III of this chapter.

2. *The Content of Christian Proclamation*

Before considering fully the problem just mentioned, it will be profitable to study the content of New Testament proclamation.

(1) *The preaching of Jesus.*—The preaching of Jesus was largely the proclamation of the kingdom of God and of his place in redemptive history. A study of the parables and sayings of Jesus reveals a concentration on the kingdom as imminent (Mark 1:14–15), as present (Luke 11:20), and as anticipated consummation (Matt. 24:25). Jesus urgently called men to repentance. He also spoke of the discipline and standards of kingdom citizenship, sought to mature spiritually the kingdom people as the new community, and proclaimed the centrality of his redemptive deed in salvation history. Without reservation, he declared his mission in the world to be that of the salvation of sinful man.

(2) *The preaching of the apostles.*—Apostolic proclamation centered in Christ—his teaching and his saving act. Such preaching united the Christ of faith and the Jesus of history. Sermons of the early church heralded the redemptive work of Christ to an unbelieving world. These sermons are discussed in chapter 3.

The content of apostolic proclamation can be summarized as follows: (*a*) In Jesus, the redemptive promises of the Old Testament have been fulfilled. (*b*) In the life, death, and resurrection of Jesus, redemptive history has reached its climax. (*c*) Jesus has been exalted as Lord and Saviour. (*d*) The presence of the Holy Spirit in the church is the sign of Christ's present power and glory. (*e*) Salvation will reach its consummation, and history terminated, at the return of Christ to judge the living and the dead. (*f*) On the basis of God's work in Christ, men should repent and commit themselves to Christ as Saviour and Lord, receiving forgiveness of their sins and the gift of the Holy Spirit. Such content has come to be known as "kerygmatic" preaching. It is based upon Paul's descriptive term *kerygma,* designating the gospel message proclaimed. We do not mean that every New Testament sermon contained all of the points just outlined. Rather, we mean that this was the essence of early preaching, the theology of New Testament sermons. Note that it is the message, not the act of preaching, that Paul has in mind: "It pleased God by the foolishness of preaching to save them that believe" (1 Cor. 1:21). Although the act and content of preaching cannot be separated, it is not the act of preaching that the world calls foolishness. It is the cross, the content of Christian preaching, which is a scandal of folly. Note also that this verse implies that there are many ways by which the gospel can be proclaimed. God uses the gospel itself, not one particular means of communicating it, to convict men.

Previous word study has established that teaching and exhortation in the New Testament usually describe address to the believing community. In contrast to *kerygma* (preaching), *didache* (teaching) describes the content of address to believers. But it is the purpose of presentation, rather than the content, which basically distinguishes between *kerygma,* the thing preached, and *didache,* the thing taught. A study of the New Testament indicates that the content of apostolic teaching was: (*a*) the words of Jesus, (*b*) ethics of the Christian life, (*c*) doctrine, and (*d*) the Old Testament. Basically, however, the content of teaching and the content of preaching were the same. Peter and John were forbidden both to speak and to teach in the name of Jesus, indicating that claims regarding Christ were the content of both speaking and teaching (Acts 4:18). In Acts 5:42, the early disciples "ceased not to teach and preach Jesus Christ." The work of Paul and Barnabas at Antioch was "teaching and preaching the word of the Lord" (Acts 15:35).

III. THE PROBLEM—IS PROCLAMATION LIMITED TO A
     GOSPEL WITNESS TO UNBELIEVERS?

The biblical language just examined creates a problem for
a definition of Christian proclamation. The New Testament
used different terms to refer to preaching and teaching. Since
it usually distinguishes between the audiences addressed in
preaching and teaching, are we to believe that the two acts
are mutually exclusive and totally different? Does proclamation mean only the witness of the gospel to unbelievers? Does
the minister preach in a New Testament sense if his sermon
is addressed to the church? Are teaching and comforting
excluded from proclamation? These questions are obviously
of theological and practical importance.

The current resurgence of biblical theology has brought
the problem into sharp focus. Many scholars insist, on the
basis of New Testament terminology, that proclamation must
be exclusively evangelistic in purpose. C. H. Dodd has been
more influential at this point than any other single individual.
In his book *The Apostolic Preaching and Its Developments,*
he contends that for the early church to preach was far different from delivering moral instruction or exhortation. He
argues that the church was interested in passing on the teaching of the Lord, but he insists that it did not make converts
thereby. "It was by *kerygma* [*the thing preached*], says Paul,
not by *didache* [*the thing taught*], that it pleased God to save
men." [4] Alan Richardson, another prominent scholar, holds
the same view. "In the New Testament, preaching has nothing to do with the delivery of sermons to the converted,
which is what it usually means today [*sic.*], but always concerns the proclamation of the 'good tidings of God' to the
non-Christian world." [5] It is clear that persons who hold this

---

[4] London: Hodder and Stoughton, 1950, p. 6.

[5] *A Theological Word Book of the Bible* (New York: The Macmillan
Co., 1957), pp. 171–72.

position narrow the scope of Christian proclamation sharply.

But the position is too emphatic. It overstates a valid New Testament truth. It is this author's belief that the biblical language makes for a valid disinction between preaching and teaching in purpose and, in some sense, content. Certainly, it defines the message of true proclamation as God's redemptive act in Christ. However, it does not force us to understand that preaching and teaching are mutually exclusive. It does not limit proclamation to evangelistic witness, though evangelism is at the heart of Christian witness. What biblical evidence have we studied to support such a conclusion?

For one thing, we have discovered that the prevalent words for proclamation, "to herald" and "to proclaim good news," do consistently refer to witness to unbelievers. However, we have also found that other words conveying the idea of preaching and proclamation are not so restricted. Some of them, as already noted, refer to an address within the Christian community.

It is true that "to herald" (to proclaim the good news) and "to teach" usually refer to an address with different objectives. This does not mean, however, that they are never used interchangeably. Matthew 4:23 describes Jesus as teaching and preaching in the synagogues of Galilee, but Mark 1:39, the companion passage, summarizes Jesus' ministry in the word "preached." Luke also refers to Jesus' total ministry in the synagogues of Galilee in terms of "preaching" (Luke 4:44). Mark 1:21-22 calls Jesus' work in the synagogue at Capernaum teaching, but, as just noted, switches the terminology to preaching in 1:39 in a description of his continuing ministry in the "next towns" and synagogues of Galilee. Although preaching and teaching may not be the same act, it would appear that Mark and Luke, in these passages, think of preaching as being sufficiently broad to include teaching. In similar fashion, Luke uses the word "preach," literally to "tell thoroughly," in Acts 17:3 to summarize Paul's ministry of explaining and reasoning with the Thessalonican Jews.

We would be hard pressed, also, to prove that "to teach" always refers to address to believers only. Unbelieving Jews are in the context of John 6:59 and 7:14. Critical Pharisees are among those "taught" in John 8:20. Teaching in Acts 21:21,28 obviously does not exclude proclamation to the unbeliever. A good illustration of the occasional interplay of the words for preaching and teaching occurs in Colossians 1:27–28. There Paul speaks of Christ "whom we preach." The word used means "to tell thoroughly," and it is one of the New Testament terms often used to mean proclamation to an unbelieving world. But Paul then uses two participles to show the means by which Christ is proclaimed. The two participles are "admonishing" and "teaching." Here proclamation clearly is large enough to include teaching.

A final evidence offered against a view that preaching and teaching are totally different in the New Testament is that, ultimately, both are concerned with God's redemptive act in Christ. Teaching explains in detail the message proclaimed. Thus, they go together and can be called proclamation. Picture the Christian life as a building. Preaching lays the foundation, and teaching builds the superstructure. Without both, the building is incomplete.

Instruction in the Christian life, then, is also proclamation if it is built upon the foundation of the redemptive message. As H. H. Farmer writes of proclamation, "If the context is always God's saving activity through history in Christ, and if the focus is the encounter of that saving activity with those who listen, then nothing that does not fog that context or blur that focus need be excluded." [6]

Our study of New Testament proclamation now leads us to draw several important conclusions: 1. Christian proclamation is the act of giving testimony to God's redemptive work in Christ. 2. Proclamation centers in the declaration of redemption to the unbelieving world. 3. Proclamation also involves teaching and exhorting believers; instructing them upon the basis of the gospel of redemption in the Christian faith; and disciplining, warning, and encouraging them. 4. Preaching in the public worship service is of the most vital concern for Christian proclamation. 5. Proclamation is not confined to public address, but involves personal witness and every other means for the propagation of the gospel.

FOR STUDY AND CLASS DISCUSSION

FOR FURTHER STUDY

1. By using the commentaries and general reference works available in your church library, study the basic content of the message delivered by each of the Old Testament prophets. Relate these messages to Christian proclamation.

2. This chapter stated that the basic content of Jesus' sermons is the kingdom of God and his place in redemption. Study several of the discourses of Jesus and list the subjects he discussed in these sermons.

FOR DISCUSSION AND CLASSWORK

1. Think back to some sermons you have heard preached in the past few months. How many of them were addressed to the unsaved? How many of them were addressed to Christians? What specific needs in your life were met by these sermons?

2. In the past, what made proclamation and teaching different for you? Have these concepts been verified or challenged by the biblical study of proclamation contained in this chapter?

CHAPTER 3

I. THE THEMES OF NEW TESTAMENT PROCLAMATION

II. THE CONTENT OF THE SERMONS OF THE NEW TESTAMENT

1. The Preaching of Peter
2. The Preaching of Stephen
3. The Preaching of Paul

3

The Gospel We Proclaim

I

THE PERSON who wished for "some wonderful place called 'the land of beginning again'" described the hunger of all reasonable men. Who doesn't look back on some page in his life and wish for a chance to rewrite it? Half of the world's misery comes from fists bruised from knocking on the door of yesterday, fingers bloodied in trying to pick the lock of a forever-sealed moment. We do not live many years before we awaken to our need for a place of beginning again.

The gospel that we proclaim affirms that, because of God's act in Christ, such a new beginning is possible. It is precisely this affirmation which makes the gospel good news. Such a glorious gospel justifies proclamation. To paraphrase James S. Stewart, the task of the church is to confront our bewildered age with the fact of Christ, to thrust upon its confusion the sure word of the cross, and to dispel man's despair with the glory of the resurrection.[1]

But the content of the gospel also defines proclamation. Christian proclamation cannot exist apart from the eternal gospel of God's provision for man's salvation through Jesus Christ. We are witnesses to a Deed. We are stewards of the Word of God. The message we have to communicate to the

---

[1] *A Faith to Proclaim* (New York: Charles Scribner's Sons, 1953), p. 11.

world does not originate with us. Our message comes from the revelation of God and remains ever the same. It must, however, be clothed in new garb in order that we can speak to man as he is in our time.

In any serious study of proclamation, the content of the gospel message must receive first attention. Otherwise, we may become more concerned with the *methods* of witness than with the *message* which we are to proclaim. The gospel we preach must be constantly examined. We must never be presumptive enough to believe that familiar statements of faith are fully adequate. They must always be tested by the Bible. Thus, we arrive at the heart of the study when, in this and the following chapter, we consider the content of the message we proclaim.

In the last chapter, we examined briefly the apostolic message. In chapters 3 and 4, we shall study this message in greater depth. Several themes for proclamation which appear in the New Testament will be set out and the New Testament sermons will be examined closely. Then, on the basis of their content and its expansion in the biblical material, a brief systematic statement of the gospel will be offered.

I. The Themes of New Testament Proclamation

Several themes of early Christian proclamation are found in the New Testament. Most often, these themes appear as objects of the verbs "to herald" and "to proclaim." Some themes apparently are general and inclusive enough to refer to the entire message which the early church preached. Among these general themes, "the gospel" or "good tidings" occur most frequently. This object of proclamation assumes various forms: "the gospel of God" (1 Peter 4:17), "our gospel" (2 Thess. 2:14), "my gospel" (2 Tim. 2:8), the "gospel of the kingdom" (Matt. 24:14), "the gospel of Christ" (Rom. 1:16), or more simply "that gospel" or "the gospel" (Gal. 2:2; Col. 1:23). In whatever form it assumes, the theme refers to all that God has done in Christ. It includes the good news of God's victorious answer to man's sin and hopelessness.

The New Testament preachers are also said to have proclaimed "the word of God" (1 Thess. 2:13). Although this theme could refer to a word *about* God, it likely means a word *from* God. Since the word of God also denotes action or deed, the theme refers primarily to God's climactic revelation of himself in Christ.

Another of the inclusive themes which describe the gospel proclaimed is "the message preached," *kerygma* (1 Cor. 15:14; Rom. 16:25). The content of this term has already been described in the preceding chapter. The main features of God's redemptive act in Christ are involved in it. A theme of similar inclusiveness is "Christ" or "the Christ" (Acts 8:5). Acts 8:5 records that "Philip went down to the city of Samaria, and preached Christ unto them." Identically, Paul asserted, "But we preach Christ crucified" (1 Cor. 1:23), and "For we preach not ourselves, but Christ Jesus the Lord" (2 Cor. 4:5). Paul uses an expansion of the theme in Ephesians 3:8 in his declaration that he was commissioned to "preach ... the unsearchable riches of Christ." These objects of proclamation describe the total gospel message, what God has done in Christ. The gospel is Christ. The Proclaimer has become the proclaimed.

Other New Testament expressions seem to carry special details of the gospel theme. These include: "the preaching of the cross" (1 Cor. 1:18); "the way of salvation" (Acts 16:17); "remission of sins" (Luke 24:47); "resurrection of the dead" (Acts 23:6); the resurrection of Jesus (1 Cor. 15:12); "preaching the things concerning the kingdom of God" (Acts 8:12); "eternal life" (John 17:2); "the word of faith" (Rom. 10:8); and "the mystery of the gospel" (Eph. 6:19). These objects of Christian proclamation make it thrillingly evident that the gospel does announce a new beginning for man.

II. The Content of the Sermons of the New Testament

Few sermons addressed to unbelievers have been preserved in the New Testament. Five sermons by Peter, Stephen's masterful defense, Paul's two sermons and two statements of defense, all recorded in Acts, comprise the group. These sermons must be considered in any attempt to reconstruct early Christian preaching and in an effort to understand the gospel that we proclaim. They, along with such summaries of the gospel as that contained in 1 Corinthians 15:1–4 and Romans 10:9, afford us a knowledge of those truths which the apostles considered essential in bringing men to salvation. No one sermon contains all of the points of proclamation defined in the last chapter. Consistently, each sermon, however, points to Christ as the fulfilment of the prophecy of a coming deliverer, who by the death imposed upon him by sinful men and through the resurrection, offers new life to all who repent and believe in him. The fact that salvation was offered to the very generation that crucified Jesus makes the power and promise of the gospel all the more evident. A brief review of these sermons will be instructive.

1. The Preaching of Peter

(1) *The sermon at Pentecost.*—Peter's first sermon (Acts 2:14–40) offers a large understanding of the gospel preached by the early Christians. It was addressed to the Jews just after the outpouring of the Holy Spirit on the disciples on the day of Pentecost. These Jews were confronted with the phenomenon of the tongues, which enabled the apostles to speak to men (or, as some believe, enabled all those present to hear and understand the gospel) of many nations in their native languages. The Jews dismissed the entire matter with the observation, "These men are full of new wine." It was then that Peter "lifted up his voice" in solemn and sober speech

to deliver his first sermon. The sermon contains six clearly discernible points of emphasis: (*a*) An explanation of the miracle. Peter refuted the charge of drunkenness and asserted that the manifestation was a fulfilment of the prophecy of Joel that in the "last days" the Holy Spirit would be poured out on all flesh, verses 14–21. (*b*) A brief reference to the life and ministry of "Jesus of Nazareth," verse 22. (*c*) An exposition of the death of Jesus as within the will of God, yet a wicked deed for which the Jews and the lawless men who crucified Jesus were responsible, verse 23. (*d*) An affirmation of the resurrection as God's act which David had prophesied, verses 24–32. (*e*) An explanation of the outpouring of the Holy Spirit, also prophesied by David, as the gift of the exalted Jesus, verses 33–36. (*f*) A call to repentance and baptism, with the assurance that those who turned to Christ would be forgiven of sin and would receive the gift of the Holy Spirit as recipients of God's promise, verse 38–40.

Since this sermon is usually regarded as a model of New Testament proclamation, several things about it should be noted. Peter made it clear that Jesus is the Messiah of promise. All that took place in the life, death, and resurrection of Jesus, Israel should have been ready to receive. Peter argued in detail that Jesus' resurrection and exaltation were in fulfilment of David's prophecies, "For thou wilt not leave my soul in hell; neither wilt thou suffer thine Holy One to see corruption" and "The Lord said unto my Lord, Sit thou at my right hand, until I make thine enemies thy footstool" (Psalms 16:10; 110:1). Further, Peter preached that in the coming of Christ and the outpouring of the Holy Spirit which followed his exaltation, the "last days" broke into history. Using the prophecy of Joel, he declared that the "new age" had dawned.

It is also important to note the central place given in this sermon to the death and resurrection of Jesus. The preacher of Pentecost drew a sharp contrast between the treatment that Jesus received at the hands of men and that which he experienced at the hands of God. While the Jews crucified Jesus by turning him over to lawless men, God raised him up and exalted him as "both Lord and Christ." Doubtless, Peter preached the cross to bring conviction to his hearers. Although the death of Jesus was within the foreknowledge and will of God, these men were responsible for his murder. Peter preached the resurrection as the birth pangs of death that guarantees the efficacy of the cross for atonement, confirms the claims of Jesus to give life, and makes the messianic kingdom a present reality.

Such a gospel calls for repentance. Those who heard Peter's sermon were struck with guilt and cried, "What shall we do?" Peter answered, "Repent, and be baptized every one of you in the name of Jesus Christ for the remission of sins" (Acts 2:38). The relation of baptism to forgiveness in the verse is understood, in light of the clear teaching of the entire New Testament, to be evidential. Peter did not use the words "baptized for the forgiveness of sins" to mean that men are forgiven of sin as a result of baptism any more than by our use of the sentence, "He was jailed for stealing," we mean that a man steals as a result of imprisonment. Forgiveness is the reason for baptism. Baptism is evidence of forgiveness. Frank Stagg translates the difficult verse well: "Repent, and let each of you be baptized in the name of Jesus Christ *on the basis of* the forgiveness of your sins." [2] The *essential* response of man to the gospel is repentance, a change of direction which involves the total person. Peter made it clear that the gifts of kingdom life are open to all whom God calls and who repent.

It should also be noted that Peter's sermon contains an emphasis on the lordship of Christ. His statement that "God hath made that same Jesus, whom ye have crucified, both Lord and Christ" asserts the total sovereignty of the Saviour.

---

[2] *The Book of Acts* (Nashville: Broadman Press, 1955), p. 62.

Let us see if these emphases are consistently presented in the other New Testament sermons.

(2) *Peter's second sermon.*—The setting of Peter's second sermon (Acts 3:12–26) is Solomon's porch. He had just healed the blind man at the gate of the Temple. The people were amazed at the incident, and Peter declared to them that the miracle was accomplished by the living presence of Christ (Acts 3:16). Once again, Peter spoke of the Jews' responsibility for the death of Jesus. He charged them with the denial before Pilate (Acts 3:13), denial of "the Holy and Righteous One" (Acts 3:14, ASV), acceptance of a murderer in the place of Jesus (Acts 3:14), and the murder of the "Prince of life" (Acts 3:15).

God's action toward Jesus, however, was quite different. He glorified his servant (Acts 3:13) and raised him from the dead (v. 15). The latter part of the sermon is a proclamation of divine generosity. Peter acknowledged that his hearers had rejected Jesus out of ignorance (v. 17), and called them to recognize that Jesus' suffering was the fulfilment of prophecy (vv. 18, 22–26) and to turn from their wickedness and repent (v. 19). He offered them the blessings of the kingdom of God, the blotting out of sin, "times of refreshing," and the coming of Christ (vv. 19–20). As F. F. Bruce states, they were being invited to "reverse the verdict of Passover Eve and to accord Jesus united acknowledgment as Messiah." [3]

The major themes of Peter's sermon on the day of Pentecost are used in the second sermon also. That Jesus is the fulfilment of prophecy is not only reaffirmed but reinforced. All the prophets are declared to have foretold the sufferings of Christ (Acts 3:18). The language of Isaiah is reflected in the descriptive term "the Holy and Righteous One" and in the account of God's glorification of his servant in verse 13. The

---

[3] *The New International Commentary on the New Testament,* "The Book of Acts" (Grand Rapids: William B. Eerdmans Publishing Co., 1955), p. 92.

second sermon also declares that Jesus fulfilled Moses' promise of the raising up of a prophet (See Deut. 18:15f.), thus tracing messianic prophecy to the patriarchs. In similar unique reference, messianic overtones are attributed to the message of Samuel and all the prophets "that followed after" (Acts 3:24, ASV). That Christ is the only hope of man's salvation comes to new emphasis in Peter's quotation of Moses, "Every soul that shall not hearken to that prophet, shall be utterly destroyed from among the people" (Acts 3:23, ASV).

The fact that the "new age" has come in Christ is strengthened in Peter's second sermon. Every blessing that Peter promised the Jews as a result of their repentance is a mark of the eschatological kingdom to which the Jews looked forward. Also, salvation is described as the fulfilment of God's covenant with Abraham. It is in Christ that the seed of Abraham is to bless "all the families of the earth" (Acts 3:25, ASV).

Consider also one theme not present in Peter's first sermon. The second coming of Christ is mentioned in the words "that he may send the Christ who hath been appointed for you, even Jesus: whom the heaven must receive until the times of restoration of all things whereof God spake by the mouth of his holy prophets that have been from of old" (Acts 3:20–21, ASV). These verses deal with the problem of delay in the consummation of the kingdom. In spite of difficulties which they present for interpretation, two things seem apparent: the consummation of the work of Jesus lies in the future; and delay in the triumphant return of Christ is not due to God's slowness, but to man's hesitance to repent. God's extended mercy, so tenderly described in Peter's address to the Jews who were contemporary with the crucifixion, accounts for man's continuing opportunity to repent.

(3) *Peter's third sermon—a defense.*—Peter's third sermon (Acts 4:8–12) occurred as a defense before the council. He and John had been arrested for teaching the people and

preaching the resurrection. They were brought before the Sanhedrin and asked by what authority they healed. In response, Peter made five contentions: (*a*) The miracle was done "by the name of Jesus Christ of Nazareth," Acts 4:8–10; (*b*) "Ye" crucified Jesus, Acts 4:10; (*c*) Whom God raised from the dead, Acts 4:10; (*d*) Jesus is the stone which "ye" rejected, but who is now the head of the corner, Acts 4:11; and (*e*) There is salvation in none other than Jesus, Acts 4:12.

No new themes are introduced in this sermon, but the theme of Christ as the fulfilment of messianic prophecy is expanded. Peter used the picture "The stone which the builders refused is become the head stone of the corner" from Psalm 118:22. This is one of the Old Testament's earliest messianic references. The fact that this prophecy was popular with early Christian teachers can be explained by Jesus' own reference to it, recorded in Mark 12:10–11.

Note also that the theme of Jesus as the only source of the salvation of God is underscored in this sermon. His name is the only name under heaven that is a saving name.

(4) *Peter's fourth sermon—a further defense.*—Peter's next defense (Acts 5:29–32) came under circumstances similar to those which produced his third sermon. He and John had been miraculously released from prison following their arrest for continued preaching and healing. They returned to the Temple to preach and were promptly brought before the council to be reminded not to speak in Jesus' name. Actually, as Luke implies in the record, the members of the council were provoked by fear that they would be held guilty for the murder of Jesus by an aroused people (Acts 5:28). The apostles' answer, doubtless voiced by Peter, was that they must obey God rather than men (Acts 5:29).

Once again Peter preached that God had raised Jesus, whom the Jews had killed by hanging him on a tree. He asserted that God had exalted his Son as a Prince and Saviour to give repentance and forgiveness of sins to Israel (Acts 5:30–31). He added, significantly, "We are his witnesses of these things; and so is also the Holy Ghost" (Acts 5:32).

The themes are familiar. Basically, they are identical with those of the previous sermons. Three interesting additions are noted, however. The guilt for the crucifixion is graphically deepened by the description of Jesus' death in the language of the curse of Deuteronomy 21:23, "He that is hanged is accursed of God." The Jews, Peter literally said, manhandled and slew Jesus in this accursed fashion. Again, the terms Peter used for exaltation add to the gospel's doctrine of the nature of Christ. God bestowed the greatest honor on him by investing him with the authority of Prince (leader) and Saviour. The terms reflect Jesus' status as the Son of man, the Saviour of the world.

Finally, Peter defended the apostles' preaching of the gospel on the grounds that they were witnesses (those who spoke from experience) of these things under the direction of the Holy Spirit, who also gives witness to the raising of Jesus.

(5) *Peter's sermon before Cornelius.*—Peter's final sermon (Acts 10:34–43) is significant for its reconstruction of the early gospel. It represents proclamation to the Gentile world. The circumstances of Peter's preaching to Cornelius and his household are familiar. God had directed Cornelius to send for Peter at Joppa, and God had dealt with his reluctant and racially conscious preacher, Peter. The apostle finally came and arose to address the congregation that Cornelius had excitedly gathered.

Peter began with the confession that he had been convinced that God shows no partiality. God opens himself to anyone who "feareth him, and worketh righteousness" (vv. 34–35). Then, Peter quickly sketched the life and ministry of Jesus as the word of good news of peace which God sent to Israel (vv. 36–39a). Peter affirmed the death and resurrection (vv. 39*b*–41), stating that the risen Christ was manifest only to those who were witnesses chosen before of God. He explained the apostles' commission to preach that Jesus is ordained of God as the judge of the living and the dead. The sermon closed with the claim that the prophets bear witness that "every one that believeth on him shall receive remission of sins."

As we compare this sermon to Peter's earlier preaching, we notice the greater attention given to the life of Jesus. F. F. Bruce and other scholars point out that the sermon has almost the same scope as Mark's Gospel. It moves from the baptism of Jesus, through his Galilean and Judean ministries, to Jerusalem and his crucifixion and resurrection. It speaks of the coming judgment and offers forgiveness through faith.

Peter went into greater detail than Luke includes in his record. Peter spoke of Jesus' healing ministry and of God's presence with him as he "went about doing good." The reason for this increased emphasis on the historical Jesus is obvious. Peter was now addressing a non-Jewish audience. Although he implied that Cornelius knew of the life of Jesus (Acts 10:36), he was careful to reinterpret that life. In all probability, this sermon is a model of the early church's proclamation to wider audiences.

Peter also emphasized heavily the universality of God's work in Christ. God will give his blessings as readily to a Gentile who desires to receive them as to a Jew (Acts 10:34–35). Jesus is Lord of all (v. 36). He is to be the judge of all (v. 42). He is the Saviour of all who believe in him (v. 43).

The end of history receives more consideration in this sermon than in much earlier proclamation. Peter proclaimed Jesus as the universal judge (Acts 10:42). Peter meant that, at the time of Jesus' second coming, he will judge both those who will be alive at that moment and all who have died. (See Acts 17:31; 2 Tim. 4:1; 1 Pet. 4:5.) Peter chose Jesus' healing of those "oppressed by the devil" as typical of his earthly ministry. This was meant to teach that the victorious kingdom to come had broken into time in the incarnation.

2. *The Preaching of Stephen*

The lengthy sermon which Stephen preached in his defense just before his martyrdom (Acts 7:2–53) is important for our study for one main reason. Stephen used Hebrew history at great length to present Christ, a device Paul used later in his sermons. Stephen had been charged with blaspheming Moses and God by stating that Jesus would destroy the temple and the customs of Moses. His defense is a moving interpretation of Christianity as universal. His survey of Hebrew history from Abraham to Solomon's Temple represented his argument against all the charges made against him. He sought to prove: (1) that God, through the patriarchs, had never limited himself to one land, Acts 7:2–16; (2) that, through Moses, it was the Jews who had blasphemed the law of Moses by turning back to Egypt "in their hearts," Acts 7:17–43; (3) that, through the Temple planned by David and built by Solomon, although God's presence had been symbolized in places of worship, God had never dwelled in "houses made with hands" Acts 7:44–50, ASV.

Stephen emphasized the familiar theme of inescapable responsibility for the death of Jesus (Acts 7:51–53). He preached that Israel's long history of idolatry, spiritual blindness, and resisting the Holy Spirit in such events as the making of the golden calf and the persecution of the prophets came to a terrifying climax in the betrayal and murder of the Righteous One. The sermon closed as his tormentors' stones began to rain upon Stephen with a further claim to universal salvation in Christ. Stephen said, "Behold, I see the heavens opened, and the Son of man standing on the right hand of God" (Acts 7:56).

The first martyr for the Christian faith thus became the only other person in the New Testament to use Jesus' own self-identification, "Son of man." This term speaks of the humanity of Jesus and emphasizes the universality of salvation in Christ. Jesus is the Son of man, and from all the races of the earth he creates the new humanity.

3. *The Preaching of Paul*

The preaching of Paul follows the same themes as those contained in earlier proclamation. C. H. Dodd states that there are only three main differences between the sermons of Paul and Peter. Paul was the first person to refer to Jesus as "Son of God" in the recorded sermons of Acts. Peter's sermons promised forgiveness of sins, but Paul was the first to state "Christ died for our sins." Thus Paul connected forgiveness specifically with the death of Jesus. Finally, Paul's proclamation was the first to state that the exalted Christ intercedes for man. Otherwise, Dodd says, Paul's preaching is identical with the earlier proclamation.[4]

Of course, Peter's silence on the three points named by Dodd should not be taken to mean that Peter did not believe or perhaps preach all three in unrecorded sermons. Paul made them explicit, however. But it is interesting to see that he did so largely in his addresses to believers, where we would expect amplification of the gospel. A brief study of four passages will demonstrate that Paul's message to unbelievers follows lines which by now are familiar.

(1) *Paul's sermon in Antioch of Pisidia.*—At Antioch of Pisidia, Paul addressed Jews and "ye that fear God," evidently a reference to some Gentiles who were in his audience. See Acts 13:16-41. In the fashion of Stephen, Paul opened the sermon with a review of Hebrew history (Acts 13:16-22). He rehearsed the mighty redemptive acts of God. He stressed God's initiative in the forming of a chosen people. Paul then proceeded to show that Jesus is the climax of God's

---

[4] *The Apostolic Preaching and Its Developments*, pp. 25-26.

redemptive act and the fulfilment of divine promises to David (Acts 13:23–37.)

In this basic discussion, Paul preached the familiar elements of the gospel message. These elements are the death of Jesus in fulfilment of the Scriptures, but with the full responsibility upon those who had him killed, and God's vindication of his Son in the resurrection, again in fulfilment of the Scriptures and confirmed by those to whom he appeared and who were his witnesses.

In this presentation of the good news, Paul made several interesting points. He spoke of the ministry of John the Baptist, especially his refusal to bear the title Messiah and his pointing to Jesus as the Promised One (Acts 13:24–25). He also made much of the burial of Jesus (Acts 13:29).

It may well be that the mention of Jesus' burial serves to make both his death and resurrection more certain. Or it may be that the reference adds to the evidence that everything about the passion of Jesus was carried out in exact fulfilment of the Scriptures. (See Deut. 21:23.) In dealing with the resurrection of Jesus, Paul, as Peter had done earlier, referred to the prophecy of David. Christ fulfilled the promises of Psalm 2:7 and 16:10. Christ, not David, is that "Holy One" who was not permitted to "see corruption."

The sermon closed with a call to faith and solemn warning toward those who refuse the gospel (Acts 13:38–41). Paul's doctrine of justification by faith becomes clear as he preached that "every one that believeth is justified from all things, from which ye could not be justified by the law of Moses" (Acts 13:39, ASV). In Christ, men are completely justified as they never could have been by Moses' law. Forgiveness through faith in Christ is not partial, but complete.

(2) *Paul's defense at Jerusalem.*—Two of Paul's sermons are actually statements of defense, the first before the Jerusalem tribunal (Acts 22:1–21) and the second before Festus

and Agrippa (Acts 26:2–23, 27). On both occasions, Paul proclaimed the gospel to unbelievers.

Before the tribunal, Paul dealt primarily with the divine origin of his mission. He spoke of his Jewish heritage (Acts 22:3), his persecution of the Christians (Acts 22:4–5), his conversion experience, and his commission to preach to the Gentiles (Acts 22:6–21). In describing his conversion, Paul recalled the words of Ananias, "The God of our fathers hath appointed thee to know his will, to see the Righteous One, and to hear a voice from his mouth" (Acts 22:14, ASV). This language underscores the gospel's claim that Jesus fulfilled prophecy and climaxed redemptive history.

The term "Just One" has Old Testament references. Not only does it depict Jesus as the great High Priest and Prophet (2 Kings 4:9), but also it declares him to be the final fulfilment of the promise of "the anointed of God," "my righteous servant" (2 Sam. 23:1–3; Zech. 9:9; Isa. 32:1; 53:11). In essence, Paul preached that he had seen and heard the risen Christ and had been ordained of God to proclaim him as Israel's Messiah and the Saviour of the world.

(3) *Paul's sermon before Festus and Agrippa.*—Much of the same ground is covered in the apostle's defense before Festus and Agrippa (Acts 26:2–23, 27). Again, Paul spoke of his Jewish background and loyalty (Acts 26:4–8), of his zealous persecution of the Christians (vv. 9–11), and of his conversion and commission (vv. 12–18). In speaking of his faithful discharge of his calling (vv. 19–23), he argued that he had preached nothing that had not been promised by Moses and the prophets. He had preached only the great hope of a Messiah who would suffer and die, be raised, and bring life to Jews and Gentiles alike.

Thus, Paul defended both himself and the gospel. He argued that Jesus is the Christ on the basis of the prophets. Just how forceful was Paul's speech is indicated in Agrippa's pathetic word after he had been challenged "Believest thou the prophets?" The king could only reply, "Almost thou persuadest me to be a Christian" (v. 28).

(4) *Paul's sermon at Mars' Hill.*—Paul's sermon at Athens (Acts 17:22–31) is of the same importance as Peter's proclamation to the household of Cornelius. It, too, represents the gospel preached beyond the Jewish community, in this instance to those skilled in the philosophic systems of ancient Greece.

The Mars' Hill sermon has been subjected to much unfair interpretation. Paul has been accused of here departing from the gospel in seeking to speak philosophically. Remembering that he next turned to Corinth, many have found evidence of repentance of the "error" in Paul's reminder to the Corinthians, "I determined not to know any thing among you, save Jesus Christ, and him crucified" (1 Cor. 2:2). He had by this time, they say, repudiated the excellency of speech and wisdom (1 Cor. 2:1) which had been tried among the Greeks.

But examination of the sermon reveals that such interpretation is unwarranted. Paul did, in fact, preach the gospel at Mars' Hill, and his sermon did meet with success, although many laughed him out of court when he spoke of the resurrection (Acts 17:32–34). Paul simply followed his principle of relevance—he began where the people were. In the case of Jews and those acquainted with the Scriptures, he began with the patriarchs and the prophets and came to Christ as the fulfilment of the Scriptures. At Athens, he began with the philosophies of his hearers and moved from them to the gospel of Christ. The practice points up a significant truth—Christ is the fulfilment of all truth. Philosophy has been the teacher which has led some to Christ. These, too, have found in him the end of their quest for truth.

Paul's point of beginning in this sermon was the altar to an unknown god that he had observed among the many shrines erected to the gods worshiped by this "very religious" people. He proposed to expound to them the god whom they worshiped as unknown (Acts 17:23). The sermon then dealt with the self-sufficiency and spirituality of God (Acts 17:24–29).

With great skill, Paul showed the fallacies of both Epicureanism and Stoicism, quoted from the poets with whom his hearers were familiar, and challenged both pantheism and idolatry. With that, he moved to the gospel and preached repentance in the name of the risen Christ who will judge the world in righteousness on a day appointed by God (Acts 17:30–31).

(5) *A summary of Paul's proclamation.*—In addition to the sermons just considered, 1 Corinthians 15:1–4 is important for understanding the gospel to be preached. This passage may be the most exact summary of the Christian proclamation in the New Testament. The sermon offers not only a knowledge of the gospel, but also a statement of the early form of the proclamation.

Paul made it clear that this was the message that he "had received" (1 Cor. 15:3), indicating a pre-Pauline proclamation. The central importance of the sermon finds expression in Paul's words, "I delivered unto you first of all" (1 Cor. 15:3, ASV). It was not merely first in time, but of first importance.

The three prime essentials of the gospel message, then, are the death, burial, and resurrection of Jesus (1 Cor. 15:3–4). About the death of Jesus, Paul made two qualifying statements and an important implication. Since the death is mentioned first in this statement of God's grace, he implied that it is at the heart of the gospel; the death of Jesus is atoning in efficacy ("died for our sins"), and the cross is in fulfilment of the Scriptures.

The burial reference doubtless further verifies the fact that

Jesus was really dead and that his resurrection is genuine. Nothing makes death more obvious nor resurrection more victorious and miraculous than burial! Paul attributed the resurrection to God; "he has been raised" is the correct rendering of verse 4. The tense of the verb also points to a continuing state. Literally, he has been raised and will not die again. And the resurrection, too, is in fulfilment of the Scriptures. Death, burial, resurrection—from these comes the good news.

Paul also summarized this gospel clearly in Romans 10:9. The "word of faith, which we preach," he writes, is centered in Jesus as Lord, indicating the sovereignty which God confirmed in Christ when he raised him from the dead. Thus, "If you confess with your mouth Jesus as Lord, and believe in your heart that God raised Him from the dead, you shall be saved" (Rom. 10:9, NASB).

This brief summary of apostolic sermons addressed to unbelievers confirms the *kerygmatic* content of proclamation claimed in chapter 2. At times, the apostles varied their message in theme and emphasis in order to speak more adequately to a particular situation. But the main features of their message remained the same. They preached Christ as the Messiah by whose death and resurrection God fulfilled his promise of deliverance. Through Christ, the new age and its blessings for those who repent and believe in him have come.

This good news of beginning again is the gospel which we are to proclaim today to men who are no less in spiritual need and darkness than those to whom Paul and Peter and the other apostles preached. In the next chapter, we shall seek a brief, systematic statement of what this redemptive deed of Christ has accomplished, and will accomplish, in human history.

FOR STUDY AND CLASS DISCUSSION

FOR FURTHER STUDY

It would be interesting to compare the content of modern preaching with that of the New Testament times. Your church library may contain several volumes of sermons by Baptist ministers and those of other denominations. Each year, G. Paul Butler edits a book of sermons he considers best, delivered by Protestant ministers. Study some of these sermons that are available with the purpose of discovering their basic gospel message.

FOR DISCUSSION AND CLASSWORK

1. Why is it necessary, in your judgment, to study the content of the New Testament sermons to build a theology of proclamation for our time?

2. Discuss some strengths and weaknesses that you observe in the content of preaching today. What suggestions do you have to offer for a more effective communication of the eternal gospel from the pulpit to our generation?

3. What differences do you see between the preaching of Jesus and the apostles? Why did these differences, if they can be found, exist? What can we learn from the preaching of Jesus which would make proclamation more effective today?

CHAPTER 4

here

4

The Gospel We Proclaim

II

THE SERMONS of the New Testament paint the content of the gospel in broad, essential strokes. Their themes were greatly expanded in their actual delivery. One can imagine Peter's emptying his memory of personal fellowship with Christ as he preached to Cornelius. He would recall the details of the Master's life and work. Or Paul, with his skilled knowledge of the Old Testament Scriptures, would add example after example in his defense before Agrippa to substantiate his claim that, in Christ, prophecy was fulfilled.

Basically, however, the apostles preached the *facts* of the gospel without comment or explanation. Interpretation of these facts occurs in the Gospels and Epistles. Such interpretation became necessary as the gospel was preached to an ever-widening audience, as time continued to separate hearers from the historical Jesus, and as the ethics and content of the Christian faith were taught.

In this chapter, we shall consider an interpretation of the gospel facts discussed previously. We are concerned with the significance of the gospel for men. We do well to remember that the New Testament presents no systematic theology, as such. Thus, systematic statements of the gospel run the risk of oversimplification on the one hand and cold lifeless dogma on the other.

Due to space limitations, this chapter will contain only the most general discussion of that which God has done in Christ and that which Christ has accomplished, is in the process of achieving, and will ultimately complete in the experience of all who commit themselves to him.

I. The Gospel—God's Act in Christ

The gospel declares that God has acted redemptively in history in Christ. Those who think of the redemptive work of the Father and of the Son as distinct are at variance with the biblical revelation. Some explanations of the atonement, for example, appear to interpret Christ's death as an appeasement toward God, as something Christ did to change the Father's intent toward men. Such concepts ignore the fact that God's love sent Jesus into the world and to the cross for man's redemption (John 3:16). As Paul writes, "God was in Christ, reconciling the world unto himself" (2 Cor. 5:19). By so writing, Paul means either that God was in Jesus for the purpose of reconciling man to himself, or that God was in Jesus personally reconciling man to himself. In either case, he argues that it was God who acted in Jesus. God moved into history in a climactic way in the birth of Jesus.

Throughout his ministry, Jesus insisted that the Father sent him into the world (John 5:37). It was with the "determinate counsel and foreknowledge of God" that Jesus died (Acts 2:23). It was God who raised Jesus from the dead (Acts 2:24) and exalted him (Acts 2:36; Phil. 2:9). In such language, the New Testament makes it clear that no part of salvation was achieved apart from an act of God. Redemption is God's act in history.

Therefore, it is wrong to speak of that which God has done in salvation as a separate thing from the saving work of Christ. These distinctions are understood only as categories which can help us to interpret the gospel we proclaim.

1. *In Christ, God's Act to Reveal Himself*

Bethlehem was not the first time that God visited with man. He once filled a desert bush with his glory. He once so filled a mountain that it quivered with the majesty of his presence. He knew Moses "face to face" (Deut. 34:10). He acted in the election and deliverance of Israel. The prophets spoke the message God revealed to them (Heb. 1:1). But in the incarnation, God both *spoke* and *acted*. In Jesus, God's redemptive act, revelation is complete. In Christ, God came into history and "tabernacled" among men (John 1:14).

The incarnation is God's complete revelation and is essential to redemption. H. H. Farmer writes that the fundamental dogma is "that in Jesus Christ God came into human history, took flesh and dwelt amongst us, in a revelation of Himself, which is unique, final, completely adequate, wholly indispensable for man's salvation. It all begins in an Event, or rather The Event, God's Event! " [1]

2. *In Christ, God's Act in Fulfilment of His Promise*

The apostolic sermons and writings testify that, in Christ, God moved in history to fulfil his promises to men. In short, the new age God promised to Israel has dawned in the life and sufferings of Jesus.

In Christ, God fulfils his promise of a new covenant. Jeremiah 31:31 refers to the "constitution" for the new community of redeemed Israel. One of the elements of this new covenant is that God will forgive the sins of his people. Not only will God forgive, but also he will regenerate man. God will write his law in man's heart, rather than upon tablets of stone. John 1:17 indicates that the promise has been kept, "for the law was given by Moses, but grace and truth came by

---

[1] *The Servant of the Word,* (New York: Charles Scribner's Sons, 1942), p. 18.

Jesus Christ." Jesus confirmed the advent of the new covenant in the institution of the Lord's Supper, "This cup is the new testament [*covenant*] in my blood, which is shed for you" (Luke 22:20; 1 Cor. 11:25). It is the blood of Christ, not the blood of sacrificial animals, that establishes the covenant of God with the new humanity.

The "new heart and new spirit" which God promised have been made possible in Christ. Paul so wrote to the Corinthians, "You are a letter of Christ, cared for by us, written not with ink, but with the Spirit of the living God, not on tablets of stone, but on tablets of human hearts" (2 Cor. 3:3, NASB). The superiority of the new covenant rests in Jesus. Hebrews 8:6 declares, "But now hath he obtained a more excellent ministry, by how much also he is the mediator of a better covenant, which was established upon better promises."

The qualities of the new age promised by God are declared to have been achieved in Christ. These qualities included the outpouring of the Spirit upon all flesh and the spiritual blessings accompanying such manifestation, described in Joel 2:28 and Isaiah 44:3. God invested these first in believers following the death, resurrection, and exaltation of Jesus (Acts 2:16f.). God promised a river of life, a figure portraying the full mercy and righteousness of God, to be known by all within the kingdom of God (Ezek. 47:22). In Christ, he kept that promise.

The peace of the new age, so vividly pictured in Hosea 2:18, has found spiritual reality in Christ (John 14:27). The promise of a resurrection (Dan. 12) is consummated in the raising of Jesus. It assures resurrection life for all who believe in him (Matt. 25:46; John 5:28–29; Acts 24:15; 1 Cor. 15:16, 20–21). The defeat of evil so dramatically promised in Isaiah 65:17f. has been achieved in the death and resurrection of Christ and awaits ultimate realization in his return (2 Pet. 3:13; Rev. 7:17; 21:1).

Paul summarizes the entire matter of God's fulfilment of his promises in Romans 15:8–9: "For I tell you that Christ became a servant to the circumcized to show God's truthfulness, in order to confirm the promises given to the patriarchs, and in order that the Gentiles might glorify God for his mercy" (RSV). The gospel is that God has acted in Christ in pursuit of his purpose to redeem and in fulfilment of his promises to men.

3. *In Christ, God's Movement Toward a Goal in History*

A result of the dawn of the new age in Christ is the assurance that God moves in history to achieve a redemptive goal. Many of the prophets conceived of God as sovereign over all the nations of the world and of the affairs of history as chapters in his ongoing purpose. See Isaiah 10:5–23. In Christ, redemptive history reaches its climax. The end of history is assured. Paul claims that "the creation itself . . . will be set free" (Rom. 8:21 NASB). In Christ, all things "consist," or are held together, and God, by the cross, is pleased to "reconcile all things unto himself; by him, I say, whether they be things in earth, or things in heaven" (Col. 1:20).

Paul's letter to the Ephesians states that the mission of the church is to bear witness to the "wisdom of God" to "cosmic powers" (Eph. 3:10). Because of its fellowship of men once separated, but now made one in Christ, the church testifies of God's purpose to gather all things together in Christ. God's purpose is the creation of a people for himself. In Christ, that goal is perfected. Salvation history, which evidently includes the redemption of creation itself, moves to its consummation. The gospel thus gives meaning and direction to history.

II. The Gospel—What Christ has Done for Man

The coming of Christ brought God's provision and man's need together. Jesus came that there might be a gospel to

preach. We shall be concerned now with a clearer understanding of the nature and significance of that redemptive
work.

No better summary of that which Christ has done for all
men who believe in him could be found than in Paul's statement of the purpose of his ministry to the Gentiles. He stated
to Agrippa that on the Damascus road Jesus commissioned
him "to open their eyes, and to turn them from darkness to
light, and from the power of Satan unto God, that they may
receive forgiveness of sins, and inheritance among them
which are sanctified by faith that is in me" (Acts 26:18). Is
this not the achievement of Christ in the redemption of any
and all men? Every phase of his life, death, resurrection, and
continuing ministry is to the end that such redemption may
be received by sinful man.

1. The Historical Jesus—
the Significance of the Life of Jesus.

The significance of the incarnation as God's revelation has
already been discussed. But there is gospel meaning other
than revelation in the earthly life of Jesus.

For one thing, the life of Jesus solidly roots Christianity in
history. God, from the beginning, has chosen to reveal himself through his mighty acts. Christianity does not rest on the
speculations of the early church. Christianity rests on Jesus
of Nazareth. The historical Jesus and the Christ of faith
cannot be separated, for without the former the latter has
no validity. W. T. Conner wrote, "Jesus was born of a virgin,
lived, died, rose from the dead. Those were not general
truths of philosophy; they were facts of history." [2] The humanity of Jesus is essential to the efficacy of the resurrection.
His coming into human hearts *now* in present encounter depends on the reality of his coming into the world *then*.

---

[2] W. T. Conner, *The Gospel of Redemption* (Nashville: Broadman
Press, 1945), p. 80.

The life of Jesus means his condescension. The Philippian letter captures the thought meaningfully: "Have this mind among yourselves, which you have in Christ Jesus, who, though he was in the form of God, did not count equality with God a thing to be grasped, but emptied himself, taking the form of a servant, being born in the likeness of men" (Phil. 2:5–7, RSV).

The life and ministry of Jesus are best portrayed in the servant image. He came to serve, not to be served (Mark 10:45). When Jesus took a towel and washed his disciples' feet (John 13:1–17), he acted consistently with the deed of Bethlehem, his birth, and Calvary, his death. By his coming into the world as man, he fulfilled the role of Suffering Servant and achieved man's salvation. It was by his poverty that we are made rich (2 Cor. 8:9). His life of service also sets an example for his followers. He taught and lived that greatness comes through service. True life comes from dying. The discovery of the real self comes from the losing of self.

The life of Jesus means also an identification. Jesus became man that he might meet the needs of men as they are. One of the most triumphant notes of the gospel is that, though sinless, he is one of us. In his baptism, Jesus identified himself with sinful humanity. He lived our kind of life, subject to the limitations of time and space, to hunger, fatigue, temptation, sorrow, and death. It was not accidental that he died between two thieves, for "he was numbered with the transgressors" (Isa. 53:12) and "he made his grave with the wicked" (v. 9).

Jesus participated fully in the life of man that man might find new life in him. Like a high priest of Israel, he represented man to God as a man. "Wherefore in all things it behooved him to be made like unto his brethren, that he might be a merciful and faithful high priest in things pertaining to God, to make reconciliation for the sins of the people. For in that he himself hath suffered being tempted, he is able to succour them that are tempted" (Heb. 2:17–18).

By reason of Jesus' identification with man, his death for man is effective. And more, man can rely upon the Mediator's understanding of life and come boldly to God through him. Man can be assured of victory in every trial of life through Jesus, "for we have not an high priest which cannot be touched with feeling of our infirmities; but was in all points tempted like as we are, yet without sin" (Heb. 4:15).

The life of Jesus means a new humanity. God began with Adam, breathed into him the breath of life, and he became a living soul made in the image of God. But that image had been scarred by man's rebellion. Man was estranged from God, and death had cast a dark pall over the race. In Jesus, God began over. Whereas he breathed into Adam and he became a living *soul*, he dwelled in Jesus and he became a life-giving *Spirit*. Adam was man made in the image of God, but Jesus was God made in the image of man.

The life of Jesus demonstrates that he is Lord. New Testament proclamation frequently refers to the lordship of Christ. That sovereignty which belongs to him by right of God's exaltation and which forms the heart of the Christian experience found expression in Jesus' life. He spoke with authority (Matt. 7:29). He was the master of nature (Mark 4:39). His miracles of healing challenged the kingdom of evil with authority and power. He boldly called men to follow him (Mark 2:14) and claimed priority in the affections of those who would be his disciples (Luke 14:26-27). Such authority substantiates the divinity of Christ and his right to the lordship to which God exalted him.

The life of Jesus is significant for the sake of his example and teachings. The early Christians did not tire of appealing to his life as the pattern of Christian character. His teachings compose the basis for an understanding of the Christian life and mission. But the life of Jesus is of much deeper significance than as an example and teacher. Jesus' life is essential to his redemptive deed; by it men are transformed to live as he taught men should live. Christ has not merely set a standard for man. He has entered into man to enable him to reach the goals set for him.

2. *The Cross—the Significance of the Death of Jesus*

How does the death of Jesus save? It was not long after Christian proclamation began that this question was raised. Consequently, the apostles, who at first had only preached the fact of the cross, began to interpret its meaning. The Gospels record that Jesus spoke much after Caesarea Philippi of the necessity of his death (Mark 8:31). It was not a necessity in the same sense that the cross was forced upon him, but a necessity born of the nature of sin, the righteousness of God, and God's purpose to save. There are indications that, as early as Jesus' baptism, he understood the cross as God's purpose for him (Mark 1:11; Psalm 2:7). Certainly, at the transfiguration his consciousness of the cross as the will of God emerges clearly. As Jesus spoke with Moses and Elijah about his death, the Voice spoke to say, "That is my beloved Son: hear him" (Luke 9:35).

Increasingly Jesus shared the details of his death with his disciples. He said that he would be "delivered unto the chief priests, and unto the scribes; and they shall condemn him to death, and shall deliver him to the Gentiles: and they shall mock him, and shall scourge him, and shall spit upon him, and shall kill him" (Mark 10:33–34). The Gospels give a great deal of space to the last week of Jesus' life, describing his death in detail. In similar fashion, an interpretation of the cross receives a prominent place in the Epistles.

During the history of theology, various theories of the atonement have emerged. This demonstrates that, because the cross is central to the gospel and remains a scandal to unredeemed human intellect, men have continued to make an effort to understand its meaning. Actually, the New Testament itself never presents a theory of the atonement as such.

All of the atonement theories of the centuries have been built
on some emphasis from the New Testament. Consequently,
each one of them emphasizes a portion of the true meaning
of Jesus' death. But no one of them adequately explains it.
No rational schema devised by finite man can ever hope adequately to explain that which is at the very redemptive heart
of God. The New Testament, however, makes several things
clear about Christ's redemptive achievement in the cross.

(1) *The cross of Jesus a demonstration.*—The so called
"moral influence," or "moral example," theory of the atonement emphasizes that, in the cross, Jesus demonstrates
redemptive truth. Actually, the cross demonstrates the black-
ness of the human heart. The one who doubts the sinfulness
of human nature, who recoils from Paul's argument that "all
have sinned, and come short of the glory of God" (Rom.
3:23) has only to stand at the cross to be convinced of depravity. Never did human sin come under such judgment. It
was as if all the malignancy of man's sin was gathered into
one moment and place. When Jesus died, man's heart was
laid bare. Man is wicked enough to do the worst to the best
that God offers.

But the love of God, the heart of God, primarily finds demonstration in the death of Jesus. He did not die to persuade
God to love sinful men. Rather, he died as he had been born
and lived, to reveal God's love for man. The cross is not the
laying on Jesus of the sins of men as upon a third party. It is
God in action in his Son, seeking to redeem men from their
sin. In an infinite mixture of holiness and mercy, righteousness and grace, Christ died to bring salvation to men. The
cross became God's great sermon on love. As the New Testament expresses it, "God demonstrates His own love toward us,
in that while we were yet sinners, Christ died for us" (Rom.
5:8, NASB); "herein is love, not that we loved God, but that
he loved us, and sent his Son to be the propitiation for our

sins" (1 John 4:10); "who loved me, and gave himself for me" (Gal. 2:20).

(2) *The cross of Jesus a deed of redemption.*—In spite of the truth that Jesus demonstrates God's love at Calvary, those who hold to the moral influence theory of the atonement stop far short of an adequate understanding of Jesus' death. The cross is a deed whereby Jesus *saves*.

The New Testament has different ways of expressing this saving deed. Jesus portrays his death as the liberation of the sinner in his use of the word "ransom" in Mark 10:45. The phrase "give his life a ransom for many" likely should be taken in a substitutionary sense. The most probable meaning is "give his life a ransom instead of (in the place of) many." The idea of substitution is prominent in the writings of Peter: "For Christ also died for sins once for all, the righteous for the unrighteous, that he might bring us to God" (1 Pet. 3:18, RSV). Again, "He himself bore our sins in his body on the tree, that we might die to sin and live to righteousness" (1 Pet. 2:24, RSV). Paul interprets the cross in a substitutionary sense: "For our sake he made him to be sin who knew no sin, so that in him we might become the righteousness of God" (2 Cor. 5:21, RSV).

Paul describes the accomplishment of the cross in several ways. He speaks of it as judgment: "For God has done what the law, weakened by the flesh, could not do: sending his own Son in the likeness of sinful flesh and for sin, he condemned sin in the flesh" (Rom. 8:3, RSV). He does not imply in this verse that God condemned Jesus. Rather, in the death of Jesus, God condemned man's sin. In the cross, God's wrath was unfurled against sin.

Elsewhere, Paul speaks of Jesus as becoming "a curse for us" (Gal. 3:13). Using a term from the slave market, he speaks of the death of Jesus as achieving redemption (Gal. 4:5; Eph. 1:17). Paul also uses the term "propitiation" or "expiation" (Rom. 3:25), meaning that Jesus "so dealt with human sin as to make it possible for God to show his favor in salvation."[3]

"Reconciliation" is a favorite expression of Paul for what Jesus accomplished: "And you, who once were estranged and hostile in mind, doing evil deeds, he has now reconciled in his body of flesh by his death" (Col. 1:21–22, RSV). See also Ephesians 2:16 and 2 Corinthians 5:18. He means much the same thing with the term "acquital" in Romans 5:18: "Then as one man's trespass led to condemnation for all men, so one man's act of righteousness leads to acquital and life for all men" (RSV).

The interpretation of the death of Jesus as sacrifice receives prominence in Hebrews. Here Jesus is declared to have offered a more excellent sacrifice for our sins. Whereas the Levitical priests had to offer sacrifice continually, Christ offered himself "once for all," thus making the complete sacrifice. Christ has now "sat down on the right hand of God," the offering perfected for all time (Heb. 7:27; 9:26; 10:12, 14). The writer also refers to Jesus as a "source of eternal salvation" and to his death as "the offering of the body of Jesus Christ once for all" (Heb. 10:10). Jesus, by the grace of God, tasted death for all men (Heb. 2:9).

The New Testament also interprets the death of Jesus to mean victory over the cosmic powers of darkness. It was through death, writes the author of Hebrews, that Jesus destroyed him who has the power of death, that is the devil (Heb. 2:14). Jesus announced his death as "the judgment of this world" in which "the ruler of this world will be cast out" (John 12:31). See also John 16:33 and 19:30. All of this points to the cross as a deed of redemption. By dying, Jesus achieved man's salvation.

(3) *The cross of Jesus a demand.*—It must never be for-

---

[3] *Ibid.*, p. 104.

gotten that the cross makes a demand upon men. Everywhere, the Christian life is interpreted in terms of the cross (Mark 8:34–35; 10:21; Luke 14:27; John 12:24). Just as there can be no Christianity without the cross, so there can be no Christian experience without a cross. Men who have been with Christ must live as he died. The Christian's cross is not some trial which he could not avoid bearing. All men, Christian or not, have trials. But only Christian men can bear a cross, for it involves the death of selfishness, involvement with sinful men who are without hope, and commitment to the redemptive purposes of God.

Effective proclamation rests upon the Christian's willingness to lose himself for the sake of others. Our churches will never be the redemptive communities they must be so long as we think more of our institutional success and self-preservation than we do of lost men. A church or a Christian must be willing to get involved with the world and, if need be, voluntarily to lose themselves for the sake of men whom God loves. Such cross bearing is demanded by the death of Jesus.

3. *The Empty Tomb—*
the Significance of the Resurrection of Jesus.

There can be no doubt that the apostles presented the resurrection of Christ as the event upon which the validity of Christianity ultimately rests. The resurrection seen as the "rock bottom" and "watershed" of the gospel is evidenced by the sermons of the apostles. Along with the death of Jesus, every sermon affirms the reality of the resurrection. What is the significance of this central act of redemption?

The resurrection assures the victory of Christ. Without the empty tomb, the cross would, at best, be an example of love and devotion to something believed in sincerely. But with the resurrection, the power of the cross becomes dramatically real. Jesus conquered death, sin, and Satan. The victory which seemed to be lost at the cross we now know was won there because God has raised Jesus from the grave.

Furthermore, the resurrection verifies the person of Jesus. All that he claimed as Saviour and Lord has been confirmed. Released from the limitations he chose when he became a man, he is now the universally exalted Christ (Acts 2:36; Rom. 1:4). These descriptions do not mean that by resurrection God made Jesus to be something he had not been before. They mean that, in putting aside the shackles of death, Jesus was released for the power and exaltation which was his by nature.

When the dawn of Christ's resurrection burst upon the night of the world's despair, victory for his *way* was also assured. And the Christian life is the way of the cross. That way, so often a scandal to the world, has been proved the conquering way. To put it in other language, we now know that good is stronger than evil.

The psalmist's despair over the apparent inequity between the righteous and the innocent (Psalm 73) and Habakkuk's struggle with the prosperity of the ungodly, so often apparent in modern man's doubt of the worth of the good, have been resolved. The empty tomb shouts, "Right will not always be on the scaffold, nor wrong always on the throne." We can also be sure that love is victor over hate, for in his resurrection Jesus' love led hate away captive.

Also confirmed is the paradox of Jesus that "whosoever shall lose his life shall preserve it" (Luke 17:33), for life is stronger than death. By the resurrection, the power of the living Christ was released to his disciples. One of the most vital evidences of the resurrection is the history of Christianity itself. The disciples, although Jesus had told them he would rise from the dead, evidently did not expect it to happen. At least, they did not linger at the tomb. They shut themselves away in a secret room. They walked the Emmaus road without hope. But suddenly, things were different. They were possessed with a new dynamic. He who had doubted, doubted no more. He who had wavered became the rock of boldness and uncompromising devotion. The Holy Spirit fell upon them. They healed the sick. They preached with power. The only explanation of such power is the living Christ in the midst of his people. "Christ is alive" was, and is to this day, the power of Christian faith, life, and witness.

The resurrection of Jesus assures the believers' victory over death (1 Cor. 15:20-28). The Christian faith never denies the reality of death. Truly, it is man's "last enemy." C. S. Lewis captures the diabolical reality of death in his classic statement of sorrow in the loss of his beloved wife: "It is hard to have patience with people who say 'There is no death' or 'Death doesn't matter.' There is death. And whatever is matters. . . . You might as well say that birth doesn't matter. I look up at the night sky. Is anything more certain than that in all those vast times and spaces, if I were allowed to search them, I would nowhere find her face, her voice, her touch? She died. She is dead. Is the word so difficult to learn?" [4]

Victory over death is not to be found in "drinking the hemlock" with courage, as did Socrates. Nor is it found in some vague Easter theme discovered in the coming of the spring, the flowers' blooming, and the plants' pushing up through the warming sod. It is not to be found in some vague belief in immortality, more philosophic in origin than biblical. Only in the resurrection can "death be swallowed up in victory." When Christ became the "firstfruits of them that slept," victory over death was assured for all who now possess resurrection life by faith. The gospel of the resurrection is that "as in Adam all die, so also in Christ shall all be made alive" (1 Cor. 15:22).

---

[4] *A Grief Observed* (Greenwich, Connecticut: The Seabury Press, 1963), p. 16. Used by permission.

III. SALVATION—PAST, PRESENT AND FUTURE

To this point, the significance of God's mighty act in Christ for human redemption has been briefly discussed. It is appropriate to close the chapter with some additional word concerning the nature of this new life in Christ which we are to proclaim to our generation.

1. Man's Response to the Gospel, the Way to Salvation

As has been noted, the primitive Christian sermons called on men to repent that they might receive the blessings of the new humanity in Christ. In other words, the gospel calls for response. In a sense, so far as personal experience is concerned, the gospel does not become the gospel until revelation is met with response. The question of the multitudes to whom Peter preached on the day of Pentecost, therefore, becomes important for proclamation: "What must we do?"

Men must repent to receive salvation. The term "repentance" needs clarification. Literally, it means a "change of mind" or "to have another mind." We must be careful to understand, however, that much more than man's intellectual processes are involved in repentance.

Repentance means an "about-face" involving the total person. Actually, to repent is to turn to God with all that a person is. Repentance means a change of mind about a number of things. Man must awaken to his moral poverty (Acts 3:26). He must be convinced that the gospel is true (Rom. 10:9) and that salvation can be possessed in none other than Christ (Acts 4:12). But repentance is more than a change of mind. Repentance involves sorrow for sin, but it is also more than sorrow. Judas repented in the sense of being concerned with, or sorry for, his betrayal of Jesus. But most certainly he did not repent in the sense of turning to God for salvation.

Repentance involves the will of man. It concerns all that man is. It is a wilful choice to turn in confession and desertion of a former way of life to God to accept his mercy and to begin a new kind of life by following Christ. One of the Bible's clearest illustrations of repentance can be found in Jonah 3. Compare this with Matthew 12:41.

The New Testament also describes man's response to the gospel as faith (John 3:16). This term, too, needs clarification. Faith involves intellectual belief and knowledge. But saving faith involves a *personal* knowledge. The best word to describe the meaning of faith is commitment. To believe in Jesus means to commit self to him.

It would be difficult to find a clearer definition of faith than Frank Stagg offers in his recent work on New Testament theology. "Faith is trust. It is openness of mind, heart, and life to God to receive what he has to give and to yield what he demands." [5] William Barclay, in much the same way, clarifies what it is to believe in Jesus: "Faith is the settled conviction that certain things are true; a commital of life to these facts; ultimately, a commital to a person." [6]

In essence, man receives salvation by turning from self and sin to Jesus, by committing trust and life to Jesus, by "following him." Somehow, we must communicate the truth that to become a Christian is neither simply a matter of emotional response nor an institutional membership. Rather, when God encounters man in the crisis of conviction, man's saving response is to turn to him in commitment of life. What else could Jesus have meant when he said to the rich ruler of Mark 10, "You lack *one thing*; go, sell what you have, and give to the poor, and you will have treasure in heaven; and come, *follow* me" (Mark 10:21, RSV, italics mine)?

Christianity is a way of life. It is a commitment to the lordship of Christ. Any other response to Jesus is a spurious

---

[5] *New Testament Theology*, (Nashville: Broadman Press, 1962), pp. 119-20.

[6] William Barclay, *Turning to God* (Philadelphia: The Westminster Press, 1964) pp. 53-55.

effort to have "cheap grace." It is an effort to have Jesus as
Saviour without commitment to him as Lord. Such a response
falls short of the true meaning of repentance and faith and
fills our churches with "baptized pagans."

2. Salvation, a Present Possession

When a person commits himself to Christ in repentance
and faith, the blessings of salvation are immediately his. The
kingdom kind of life breaks into his life here and now. The
New Testament uses several terms to describe the work
which Christ, through his death and resurrection, achieves
in man when he becomes a Christian.

In Christ, man receives eternal life (John 3:36). The term
does not refer to endless life, primarily, although this is involved in it. Eternal life is basically a dimension of life. It is a
new life, a kingdom kind of life, God's life. It can be described as life received and lived under the sovereign lordship of Christ. Man's constant search for meaningful life
ends in Jesus. The possession of such life is in the present
moment. It does not await the Christian's translation into
heaven, for "whosoever believeth in him should . . . have
everlasting life" (John 3:16). Because of God's redemptive
deed in Christ, that kind of life which belongs to the future
consummation comes to the believer now.

The terms "new birth," "new creation," and "regeneration"
speak of much the same thing. They describe man's salvation
as the creative work of God (John 1:12–13; Eph. 2:8–9) and
as a revolution in human nature (2 Cor. 5:17; Titus 3:5).

The New Testament often describes salvation as a liberation or deliverance (Col. 1:13). At the cost of "his own blood"
(Heb. 9:12), Jesus has set man free from the slavery of sin.
The word "redemption" expresses the same concept of deliverance from the imprisonment of sin and the law.

Closely akin to this concept, forgiveness frequently describes the blessings of salvation achieved by Christ (Acts 2:

38; 10:43; 1 John 1:9). When a man is forgiven of his sin, the barriers standing between him and God are removed. The man is restored. A similar meaning of salvation is found in the term "reconciliation" (2 Cor. 5:18; Eph. 2:16). When God reconciles man to himself, he overcomes the barrier between man and God erected by man's sin.

It should be noted that reconciliation to God means reconciliation between men also (Eph. 2:13-22). Paul's treatise on the destruction of the middle wall of partition between Jew and Gentile condemns our effort to claim reconciliation with God while we live unreconciled to one another. Modern Christians should be careful that their attitudes toward other men not harm their witness to God's power to reconcile all men to himself and to one another.

Man's salvation also means his present justification (Acts 13:39; Rom. 8:33; 1 Cor. 6:11; Gal. 2:16). Paul especially delighted to use this expression, borrowed from the courts of law, which signifies that man, by grace, receives a favorable standing before God. He writes in Romans 4:25, "Jesus was put to death for our transgressions and raised with a view to our being made righteous." Justification means an imputed righteousness. In Christ, we who have no right to do so stand before God and are accepted by him.

In salvation, men are also sanctified. The primary idea here is separation or holiness. In Christ, believers are "set apart," consecrated to God's will and design. The language of 1 Corinthians 6:11, "You were washed, you were sanctified," makes it clear that sanctification is a present possession of the Christian. One New Testament scholar says that the Christian life is "a progress in, . . . not a progress toward a sanctification." [7]

Salvation means also a "quickening" from the dead, a resurrection. In the Bible's most eloquent presentation of the miracle of redemption, Paul writes, "Even when we were dead

---

[7] Alan Richardson, *A Theological Word Book of the Bible* (New York: The Macmillan Co., 1950), p. 218.

through our trespasses, [he] made us alive together with Christ (by grace you have been saved), and raised us up with him, and made us sit with him in the heavenly places in Christ Jesus" (Eph. 2:5–6, RSV).

In redemption, man achieves the selfhood which God intends for him. It is popular to say that, when one becomes a Christian, he *dies* to self, he *loses* self. How much more accurate to say that as he dies to selfishness and commits his will to the lordship of Christ, the Christian *gains* the person he was created to be. One of man's most pressing questions concerns the meaning of his person. His search for selfhood ends in Christ. When one commits himself to Jesus, he *finds* himself. At last, he is free to be a person.

All of this Jesus has accomplished for man. This and much more man possesses *now* in his salvation.

3. *Salvation, a Continuing Process*

There is a sense in which believers *have been* redeemed. There is another sense in which they *are being* saved. The New Testament has much to say about the continuing work of Christ. He makes intercession for men at the "right hand of God" (Rom. 8:34; Heb. 7:25). The Holy Spirit mediates the presence of Christ in the human life to intercede in the believer's prayer (Rom. 8:26), to guide him into all truth (John 16:13), to be alongside him to guide his steps (John 14:16), and to empower the witness of the Christian church (Acts 2:14f.).

Sanctification has begun and, in one sense, is accomplished by Christ in the believer at the time of salvation. But the Christian is in the process of being saved by God's continual redemptive ministry in his life as he grows "unto the measure of the stature of the fulness of Christ" (Eph. 4:13).

Paul captures the concept of our continuing salvation in 1 Corinthians 15:2. There he describes the gospel as that "by which you are saved." The tense of the verb indicates that salvation is present and continuous. As Leon Morris wisely writes, "Salvation is not exhausted by a man's experience when he first believes. It is something that goes on from strength to strength and from glory to glory." [8]

4. Salvation, a Future Certainty

Many efforts have been made to identify the key motif by which the Bible and the gospel may be interpreted correctly. There can be little doubt that the key to a unified understanding of the Scriptures is in the concept of redemptive history. The Bible is eschatological to the core—that is, it looks to an age to come.

The Old Testament records the mighty acts of God in human history as he moved toward his design to redeem men. As chapters 3 and 4 have continually reemphasized, the gospel of the New Testament declares that in Christ these Old Testament acts and promises are fulfilled. Yet, the New Testament also looks to the future. Jesus preached both that the kingdom is at hand and that the kingdom is in the future.

The meaning of both a present and a future kingdom is exactly this: In Christ, the future age is already broken into time, so that salvation no longer belongs to a hope for the future. But the full experience of redemption remains for the future. The kingdom is inaugurated. It already exists in the hearts of believers (Luke 17:21). It will be consummated at the triumphant return of our Lord and at the end of history. The gospel, then, is concerned with a "holy history" which God is working out in human history.

God's act in Christ is the climax of that holy history. The war has been won; only the battles, which nevertheless are very real, remain. The enemy was defeated at Calvary and in the garden of resurrection. Yet he battles on, unaware of his

[8] R. V. G. Tasker, ed., *The First Epistle of Paul to the Corinthians*, "The Tyndale New Testament Commentaries" (Grand Rapids: Wm. B. Eerdmans Publishing Co., 1958), p. 204.

defeat, until that day when he will be vanquished. The blessings of salvation which belong to the Christian here and now are foretastes in time of his future salvation. They are guarantees that "He who began a good work in you will perfect it until the day of Jesus Christ" (Phil. 1:6, NASB).

When the message of the Bible is grasped under this theme, the gospel takes on even a greater dimension of good news. Think of the victory of it: In Jesus, the future broke into the present. Every time Jesus healed the afflicted, he affirmed the certainty of that time when there shall be no more disease. When he raised the dead, and especially by his own resurrection, he guaranteed that the day approaches when death shall no longer reign over man. Isaiah's hope is certain to be consummated: "No more shall there be in it [*Jerusalem*] an infant that lives but a few days, or an old man who does not fill out his days, . . . they shall build houses and inhabit them; they shall plant vineyards and eat their fruit. They shall not build and another inhabit; they shall not plant and another eat; for like the days of a tree shall the days of my people be" (Isa. 65:20–22, RSV).

Every broken relationship restored by Christ spoke of that future time when kingdom peace will come, a peace that will cause "the lion to lie down with the lamb" and wars to cease. His every victory over nature depicted that coming kingdom when all things, both in heaven and in earth, will be gathered up in Jesus. Every possession of the Christian now predicts that the future consummation of God's kingdom, which has already broken into time, is assured. We have the privilege and responsibility to proclaim this gospel to a broken world.

These last two chapters have described the content of Christian proclamation. By an examination of New Testament preaching and by a statement of the significance of God's redemptive act in Christ, we have sought to understand the meaning of the gospel. We must now consider how this good news can be shared with others in our time.

FOR STUDY AND CLASS DISCUSSION

FOR FURTHER STUDY

1. Because of the limitations of space, this chapter has not exhausted a discussion of the various biblical descriptions of the nature of salvation. Such terms as eternal life, the new birth, redemption, forgiveness, justification, sanctification, and resurrection have been discussed. Are there other biblical descriptions that explain still other facets of man's salvation experience? A careful study of the New Testament and of books on Christian doctrine will make interesting research into the subject.

2. Since the cross is of such essential importance to the gospel we proclaim, a study of the classic theories of the atonement would be profitable. The following books are helpful for such a study:

W. T. Conner, *The Gospel of Redemption* (Nashville: Broadman Press, 1945).

W. T. Conner, *The Cross in the New Testament* (Nashville: Broadman Press, 1954).

L. W. Grenstead, *A Short History of the Doctrine of the Atonement* (London: Longmans, Green and Co., 1920).

Frank Stagg, *New Testament Theology* (Nashville: Broadman Press, 1962).

FOR DISCUSSION AND CLASSWORK

1. How do the concepts presented in this chapter help to explain the basic unity of the biblical message? What can be done in our preaching and teaching to create a better understanding of the nature of the biblical revelation?

2. The closing section of this chapter proposed that every victory of Jesus over evil guarantees the certainty of the future triumph of the kingdom of God. What hope does the gospel thus give to men in the crises of our time? Think of some people you know who need this good news desperately.

3. Do you think the average person understands the biblical terminology that describes the salvation experience? If your answer is no, what do you think can be done to make the content and meaning of the gospel more understandable today?

CHAPTER 5

5

Proclamation
Through Preaching

PAUL'S LAST CHARGE to Timothy, his tenderly loved son in the ministry, was to "preach the word" (2 Tim. 4:2). Paul wrote an eloquent tribute to those who "preach the gospel of peace" and thought of himself as a herald of God. Thus, he did not hesitate to urge his young disciple to give preaching first place. We have studied the nature and content of Christian proclamation. As we turn to the means by which the gospel can be communicated, the same emphasis on the primacy of preaching will be made.

Preaching may be understood virtually to be synonymous with proclamation so that preaching includes many ways to bear witness to the gospel. Yet, preaching will be limited in this chapter to mean the public proclamation of the gospel, usually in the public worship service. It is exactly in this sense that preaching is primary.

Spiritual renewal in the church demands a rediscovery of preaching by minister and congregation alike. Such a discovery cannot occur apart from an adequate theology of preaching. Pursuing this theology, this chapter deals with the primacy of preaching, with preaching as a redemptive history, and with several practical suggestions for a revival in preaching. Consider, first, the reasons why the preaching hour offers the greatest potential for witness.

I. THE PRIMACY OF PREACHING

Many would deny that preaching comes first in Christian proclamation. Some are honestly convinced that the sermon is less effective for the propagation of the gospel than many other means of communication. They remind us of the many changes in culture which make a traditional sermon obsolete. It cannot be doubted that preaching needs the "fresh air" which changes in style and sermonic form have to offer, but it is something else to argue that preaching itself can ever be replaced. Many church attenders think of the sermon as something to be lived through, as somewhat apart from worship.

The cure for such an attitude may be in the ancient formula for waking sleepers in church. An usher needs to take a pointed stick and jab the preacher! Preaching needs to be improved, but it can never be eliminated. Every Christian must "preach." But this emphasis must never be made at the expense of the uniqueness of a uniquely called spokesman of God and his place in the pulpit to publicly proclaim the gospel. Every legitimate means of communication of the gospel to our world must be used, but pulpit preaching must remain at the vital center of all Christian proclamation.

1. *For the Advance of Christianity*

The centrality of preaching in the ministry of Jesus cannot be doubted. He inaugurated his mission in an announcement which magnified preaching. He had been anointed, he said, to "*preach* the gospel to the poor," to "*preach* deliverance to the captives," to "*preach* the acceptable year of the Lord" (Luke 4:18–19). As J. B. Weatherspoon writes, "from the day when he returned from the wilderness in the power of the Spirit, proclaiming the kingdom of God and urging men to repent, until that day when he stood and cried, 'If any man thirst, let him come to me and drink,' his ministry was preeminently a pageant of preaching." [1]

Jesus committed the same kind of ministry to his disciples. He selected and trained them that he "might send them forth to preach" (Mark 3:14). Paul's conviction concerning the place of preaching in his ministry becomes apparent in his reminder to the Corinthians, "Christ sent me not to baptize, but to preach the gospel" (1 Cor. 1:17). The place of preaching in the early church has been well established in our previous review of apostolic sermons and their content.

Wherever preaching has received the significance sanctioned by the New Testament, evangelical Christianity has advanced. Powerful preaching has accompanied a strong sense of biblical authority. Where the Bible has been read by the people, where ministers have been servants of the Word, there preaching has been dynamic, and evangelical Christianity has found renewal and growth.

Consider the Reformation. No other period in Christian history shows the integral relationship of preaching and Christian advance more clearly than this period. Historians rightly claim that the great achievements of that mighty revolution were, for the most part, the result of preaching. The priority of preaching as the Reformers exposed the Bible to the people was a powerful sledge to break the binding chain of a dead church authority.[2]

The Reformation, on the other hand, and the renewal of culture to which it was in part a debtor, produced a renewal in preaching. John Broadus summarizes the beneficent effects of the Reformation on the pulpit. There appeared a new emphasis on preaching as the vital element in Christian worship and life, the exposition of the Scriptures which revived biblical preaching, the rise of doctrinal preaching, and an em-

---

[1] *Sent Forth to Preach* (New York: Harper & Bros., 1954), p. 16.
[2] *cf.* Dargan, *A History of Preaching*, I, 366f.

phasis on justification by faith as central to the gospel.[3] The Reformers believed in the primacy of preaching because they believed in the Word of God as a proclaimed Word. They could not conceive of a true sermon apart from the exposition of the Scriptures. With such preaching, they replaced the elaborate ritual of the Catholic mass.

The Reformation remains a classic confirmation of evangelical Christianity's identity with preaching. So vital was this period for Christian renewal that today's emphasis on a biblical theology of proclamation largely is a neo-Reformation emphasis.

2. *For Christian Worship*

Vital to a Reformation concept of preaching is the truth that preaching is primary in worship. Both those who think of the sermon as *all* of worship and those who exclude preaching from worship are in error.

Worship means man's total, obedient response to God's grace. Worship can exist, then, only when God speaks to man in a revelation of what he has done in Jesus Christ for human redemption. At this point, the proclamation of the gospel becomes the center of worship. Through preaching, God speaks and men become aware of his redemptive love. God proclaims through the preacher, and man listens. This is the very heart of worship. And when response follows preaching, proclamation finds its completion.

Preaching is worship for the preacher, also. The sermon should be the minister's act of devotion to God. P. T. Forsyth explains it thus: "It is the Word of the Gospel returning in confession to God who gave it. It is addressed to men indeed, but in truth it is offered to God. Addressed to men but offered

---

[3] *Lectures on the History of Preaching* (New York: A. C. Armstrong, 1889), pp. 113-18.

to God—that is the true genius of preaching." [4] Such a concept ought to impel every minister to bring his best in preparation and energy to the pulpit. Here, more than in any other area of his work, he brings his oblation to God. Since the minister preaches on behalf of the church, the sermon also is the church's response to God. Perhaps this explains further why the spiritual vitality of a congregation may be measured accurately by the strength of its pulpit.

3. For All Other Means of Proclamation

Christian proclamation may be done in many ways. Yet the preaching hour contains the greatest potential for Christian witnessing available to the church. Two facts, both theological and functional, substantiate this claim.

The New Testament gives priority to the concept of the church as a community of believers called out to witness. In contrast to individual Christians dispersed here and there, the proclamation done within the Christian community must have the priority. The communion of faith is nowhere recognized so clearly as in preaching. Proclamation through personal witnessing is both biblical and mandatory. But personal witnessing must not be allowed to cloud the importance of preaching as the proclamation of the people of God to the world.

Preaching remains first among all means of proclamation because of its potential for a clear interpretation of the gospel. No other means of proclamation can equal the preacher's opportunity to clarify the gospel. He not only witnesses most effectively to the world himself. He also, through his instruction of the believing community, enables them to do their work of proclamation. Preaching strengthens all other forms of witness.

---

[4] *Positive Preaching and the Modern Mind* (Grand Rapids: Wm. B. Eerdmans Publishing Co., 1907), p. 66.

II. PREACHING AS REDEMPTIVE HISTORY

The renewal of the primacy of preaching in our time will come only when ministers and churches gain a new insight into the sacredness of preaching. Preaching is not merely a man talking about redemption. Preaching participates in redemptive history. Four expressions of this truth will make this clearer.

1. *Preaching and Revelation*

The revelation of God finds completion in the response of man. Revelation is complete in God's manifestation of himself in his Son. But a man must know God for himself, since revelation is personal. He must personally respond to that which God has done in Christ. Thus, in regard to God's making his redemptive act in Christ known to man, revelation continues. The goal of God's self-disclosure is man's response of faith and his ensuing salvation. In this sense, revelation is completed in man's response. As a recent book on the theme of man's response to God states it, "Speaking of revelation apart from response would be as speaking of sound without the ear to hear, or sight without the eye to perceive." [5]

The work of illumination expresses what the idea of continuing revelation implies—the work of the Holy Spirit. This fact must remain clear. The Holy Spirit illumines the mind of man by the interpretation of the Word of God through preaching. It is not the preacher who continues revelation. Nor is his sermon equal as revelation to the Prophets or the Gospels. Rather, when the minister preaches the Word of God, the Holy Spirit uses him and his sermon to interpret for the hearer what God has done in Christ and to seek the hearer's response in commitment.

---

[5] Roy L. Honeycutt, *Crisis and Response* (New York: Abingdon Press, 1965), p. 9.

We might think of the Word of God in three categories and in this order: the revealed Word, Christ; the written Word, the Bible; the spoken Word, proclamation. The experience of God's Word for an unbeliever may well occur in reverse order, however. Through the spoken Word he encounters the written Word, and through the written Word he encounters Christ and redemption. Thus, by the pleasure of God, preaching participates in redemptive history. Through public proclamation the Holy Spirit makes God's redemptive act in Christ known to man in our time.

2. *God Speaking in Preaching*

Another way of expressing the same concept of preaching as redemptive history is to underscore the fact that God speaks through man in preaching. This is a presumptuous claim to make. But preaching remains a presumptuous act. This fact gives it its sacredness. It astounds and humbles a man to think that God may speak to other men through him. Yet, this is what happens in true preaching.

The New Testament speaks often of the apostles' belief that God speaks through preaching. In his sermon before Cornelius, Peter stated that, in the Word proclaimed throughout all Judea concerning the person and work of Jesus of Nazareth, God preached (Acts 10:36). In Ephesians 2:17, in a reference to proclamation by the apostles, Paul states that Christ "came and preached peace to you which were afar off." He affirms the same truth in 1 Thessalonians 2:13. He declares that through his and his co-laborers' proclamation, his readers "received the word of God."

Every preacher has experienced the incomparable joy of being used as a spokesman for God. Because he knows that there have been times when God has spoken through him, he is painfully aware of those times when he seems to speak only for himself. Sensitive congregations know when God speaks through the preacher. No preacher has the power to compel God to speak in his sermon. But to the praise of God's grace and to the complete humility of the preacher, God can speak through preaching.

Indeed, God does speak when true preaching occurs—not by fiat of the preacher, but by God's initiative of grace. This fact should add great expectancy to preaching for ministers and congregations alike. Charles Hadden Spurgeon never forgot that through the stumbling words of a man, Christ spoke to him and melted his heart. He never preached without believing that Christ could speak to someone else through him. It is no wonder that he preached with poise and power. Preaching participates in redemptive history because God speaks through the preacher.

3. *God Acting in Preaching*

In preaching God acts. This is another way to describe preaching as redemptive history. True preaching is far more than a man talking—it is a part of God's act to redeem men.

This statement must be understood. It does not mean that preaching reenacts God's unique redemptive deed in the crucifixion and resurrection of Jesus Christ. Rather, it means, in the words of J. B. Weatherspoon, that the preacher becomes in proclamation a "partner with God in his saving activity." [6] The responsibility for the salvation of men rests heavily upon the herald of God. Unless the cross and resurrection become present reality through Christian proclamation, they remain only past history.

One scholar clarifies the point forcefully: "It is by preaching that God Himself makes past history a present reality. The cross was, and will always remain, a unique historical event of the past. And there it will remain, in the past, in the books, unless God Himself makes it real and relevant to men today. It is by preaching . . . that God accomplishes this

---

[6] *Sent Forth to Preach, op. cit.,* p. 93.

miracle." [7] Through preaching, God continues to offer himself to all who will believe. Through preaching, he not only speaks, he acts.

4. *The Age of Preaching*

God's purpose in history is to create a people for himself. This is the central meaning in all history. This "holy history" has been in process within history and came to a climax in God's redemptive act in Christ. In the cross and resurrection, the victory of God's purpose was achieved. But, as the gospel of New Testament proclamation clearly states, that victory has not yet been fully realized. It will become apparent at the triumphant return of Christ.

In the interim between the resurrection of Christ and the consummation of history, the redemption achieved in Christ is to be preached to the world. The gospel is a proclaimed gospel. It must be told, person by person, year by year, if it is to be good news to men. Preaching proclaims good news until that day when God's purposes will be consummated and holy history will reach its fulfilment. Because preaching has been ordained of God to proclaim the gospel "between the times," it participates in the redemptive history that began in creation, that was climaxed in the death and exaltation of Christ, and that will be fully realized in the "last days" when the kingdom that has already broken into time will be consummated.

III. THE CONTENT OF PREACHING WHICH PARTICIPATES IN REDEMPTIVE HISTORY

Not everything which has been called preaching can qualify as the act of holy history, which preaching has just been described to be. Throughout the discussion, it has been said that only in *true preaching* does Christ speak.

---

[7] Stott, *The Preacher's Portrait* (Grand Rapids: Wm. B. Eerdmans Publishing Co., 1964), p. 53.

1. Preaching to Be Gospel Centered

By any theological or biblical definition of preaching, the proclamation of the redemptive deed must be the heart of any true sermon. Preaching must be *kerygmatic,* that is, it must center, as did apostolic preaching, in Christ.

This does not mean that every sermon must contain all of the emphases of the sermons in the New Testament. It does not mean that every sermon must deal with the cross as such. But it does mean that every true sermon must contain the *gospel.* It must bear the good news of grace. After all, there is a difference between "good advice" and "good news." Many sermons, because they bear no relationship to God's redemptive act in Christ, are humanistic and philosophical in nature. They cannot be called biblical sermons. True preaching always proclaims the gospel.

The biblical evidence for this claim is found in apostolic preaching. Some protest that while this evidence may very well be found in the preaching of Peter and Paul, it ignores the preaching of Jesus. He did not always preach gospel sermons in the sense of centering his preaching in his redemptive act. Is Christ not our model for preaching? The protest ignores the fact that Jesus himself became the gospel that all Christians who come after him are to proclaim.

Jesus ministered and died that there might be a gospel to preach. Beginning at Pentecost, Christ became the gospel. The Proclaimer became the proclaimed. One would be hard pressed also to prove that the preaching of Jesus and apostolic proclamation are sharply at variance. Jesus preached the kingdom of God and called men to repentance. The apostles preached the Christ-event as the coming of the kingdom into time and called men to repentance.

Gospel preaching is more than evangelistic preaching. It is true that proclamation first announces the gospel to an unbelieving world. But gospel sermons can have many objectives. They support the Christian life, they teach the faith, they call for consecrated service, they celebrate God, and they seek to bring men to live the life of the kingdom. Some deny the Christian minister's responsibility to speak to the social and ethical issues of his time on the basis that such preaching is not "gospel" preaching. This denial has no basis in biblical or theological fact.

It would be interesting to study how many gospel facts Paul preached for the specific purpose of moral exhortation. All gospel sermons, evangelistic, life situational, or ethical must be *based* on redemption. Preaching means the proclamation of grace and its implications for life. Nothing else from the pulpit can be theologically defined as proclamation. It is "the foolishness of the thing preached" which Paul declares to be used of God to save men. The "thing preached" is Christ.

2. *Preaching to Be Biblical*

The sharing of "religious ideas" need not be biblical. But preaching means that, because God speaks through men to men in judgment or grace, it participates in redemptive history. Thus, preaching must be biblical. The Bible is the unique authoritative source of knowledge about what God has done in Christ. The Scriptures are not only indispensable to us for our knowledge of revelation, but they also are the elect way God chooses to speak his Word to us today. Therefore, if preaching must be gospel centered, it must also be biblically centered.

Biblical sermons, however, may take many forms. They do not require that the minister read a text at the beginning of every sermon. Nor does the mere use of biblical words make a sermon biblical. Such preaching can lack the dynamic imagination of the Scriptures; it can even miss the intent and spirit of the biblical message by substituting "letter" for "spirit." Biblical preaching means that the sermon communicates the truth of a biblical passage or theme. In the truest sense of the word, the preaching which participates in redemptive history "exposes" the meaning of the Scriptures.

Our generation has seen its share of humanistic sermons that gain their content from "ideas" structured without reference to a biblical text. Sermons unrelated to biblical authority or which corrupt the meaning of the Bible are no sermons at all. They may be religious essays. But all preaching that participates in redemptive history proclaims the redemptive deed in Christ through the Scriptures. This preaching demands of the preacher the most diligent, honest, and trustful reliance upon the biblical text.

3. *Preaching to Be Relevant*

Much preaching fails as proclamation because it is not exciting. It is not contemporary. The problem of Christian proclamation has always been: How can the eternal Word be communicated to the changing and contemporary mind? Two extreme views offer solutions to this problem.

One view assumes that response is not involved in proclamation and is of no importance to the preacher. The preacher may believe that the mere repetition of the message, without personal involvement or without any effort to gain response from his hearers by the use of exciting and creative style, is sufficient. The message repeated will create its own relevance, this view holds.

The other extreme view assumes that to be relevant the preacher must change the symbols of the Scriptures and reflect embarrassment with all biblical language by stripping it from the sermon so as to bring the redemptive message into confrontation with modern man. Both views offer worthy insights, but neither is an adequate solution to the problem of modern communication.

A better suggestion is to study the text until the Word of God contained in it has gripped the preacher's heart. Then he must sit before his people until he discovers where the truth of the text meets the life of his own time. This application may be communicated through contemporary sermon forms and style. Then, the proclamation of the preacher has both the authority of the biblical Word and the communication value of encounter with contemporary need.

No choice has to be made between true biblical preaching and relevance. The Bible is relevant, eternally so. But the preacher must not make it irrelevant by his lack of participation in the imagination, vitality, and dynamic quality of biblical truth. Sermons should be neither shallow existentialism without biblical authority nor arid history lessons without the excitement of the gospel's word to life here and now.

IV. THE ROUTE TO A REVIVAL IN PREACHING

The theology of preaching which this chapter has presented as biblical demands rededication to the primacy of preaching by our people. The renewal is long overdue in a century of decline in the spiritual power of the pulpit.

1. *For Congregations—a New Understanding*

A revival in preaching demands new awareness from all church members. The sermon needs support for its purposes from the other ministries of the church. It is all too obvious that preaching is not in good standing with many congregations. In study groups and through the existing training organizations in the church, congregations can gain an understanding of the ministry of the pastor and of the purpose of the sermon. Our people need to understand the minister's role as a servant of the Word. They need wide knowledge of the principles of biblical interpretation and of the various sermon forms for use in biblical preaching. They need to sense the redemptive potential in every worship service.

This new awareness of preaching by church members will

result in their assisting the preacher in his effort to magnify the office of preaching. Congregations will begin to make it possible for the pastor to major in preaching. They will understand that preaching demands time for preparation. Churches can give pastors the time for disciplined study and spiritual preparation which genuine preaching demands. Furthermore, an informed church will much more likely grant its pastor the freedom to speak what he believes God speaks. New respect for preaching by church members in the pew will lead to new power in preaching in the pulpit.

2. *For Ministers—a New Dedication*

In the final analysis, however, renewal in preaching in our time primarily depends upon the discipline and dedication of those who preach. The image of the minister as a pastor-administrator, although fruitful in many ways, may rob the preacher of his devotion to his primary calling. The modern minister must fill many roles. He must be a counselor, a teacher, an administrator, and in them all he must be a *servant*. But if preaching is the act of redemptive history which this chapter contends that it is, it calls for the primacy in the minister's life.

The realization that much more than a public speech occurs when he stands to preach on Sunday will make any sincere man ashamed to bring an unprepared mind, a tired body, and a prayerless heart to the pulpit. The serious preacher will not come to the hour of proclamation happily when he has spent more time the previous week in administration than he has spent in sermon preparation. He will refuse "easy" preaching which costs little in serious exegesis of the Scriptures and in the courageous search for the mind of God. He will be the servant of the Word. He will be continuously busy in his development of new sermon forms and of dynamic and exciting expressions of the gospel, that he may be used of God to win the response of his hearers.

A recent suggestion that preachers ought to be taken off mailing lists, deprived of telephones and ecclesiastical success sheets, flung into studies, given a Bible, and tied to the pulpit until they preach the Word of the living God may appear extreme. But at least the direction is right. Preaching costs. It is never easy. Ministers must regain an understanding of its centrality and true content and purpose and become servants of the Word, announcing redemption to men where they live today. Then, spirit and usefulness will return to the pulpit, and the people will "look up and be fed."

FOR STUDY AND CLASS DISCUSSION

For Further Study

1. It was suggested in this chapter that church members become acquainted with the various forms of biblical sermons. What books in homiletics (preaching) are available in your church library?

2. Baptists have been known for their attention to preaching. Make a brief study of the history of Baptist preaching. Two collections are of particular benefit for such a study: *Baptist Advance*, Davis C. Woolley, ed., (Nashville: Broadman Press, 1964), pp. 419–45; and *Encyclopedia of Southern Baptists* (Nashville: Broadman Press, 1958), II, 1103–10.

For Discussion and Classwork

1. Discuss some of the strengths and weaknesses of Southern Baptist preaching. How could you become more involved in making your pastor's preaching effective?

2. It has been claimed in this chapter that, in order to become proclamation, preaching must be related to God's redemptive act in Christ. How could sermons on controversial and life situation issues be gospel centered?

3. How could the average Christian be made to understand the importance of preaching?

4. Suggest some ways in which preaching should strengthen all other forms of Christian witness.

CHAPTER 6

6

Proclamation
Through Personal Witness

A TEN-YEAR-OLD BOY came forward in a revival service in his church to register a decision of Christian commitment. Deeply moved, he explained to his pastor, "I am disturbed because, since I became a Christian, I have only spoken to two people about Jesus." This sensitive young Christian understood his vocation to be that of a follower of Christ! He was convinced that to answer God's call to salvation is to become involved in God's redemptive mission in the world. The conviction he expressed needs to be shared by all Christians.

In whatever place and way Christ breaks through human personality to encounter other persons, proclamation occurs. The public proclamation of the gospel through preaching remains primary for the Christian witness. But beyond that, every Christian, as a servant of the Word, must bear witness to the gospel in the world.

This chapter will be concerned with proclamation through personal witness. We shall first take note of several contemporary challenges which confront Christian proclamation today. Then, we shall attempt to see that only by personal witness can modern Christianity make its most vital advance. Finally, we shall consider several suggestions for making proclamation a responsibility of every Christian.

I. WITNESS—THE CHURCH'S CONTEMPORARY CHALLENGE

From the outset, we have insisted that proclamation is the Christian mission. God is not only at work *with* his people. He is at work *through* his people *in* the world. The commission of Jesus to his disciples makes the task of the Christian church clear. He commanded his followers to "disciple" all nations (Matt. 28:19) and decreed that they were to be his witnesses "to the end of the earth" (Acts 1:8). Southern Baptists share with all Christians this task in a rapidly changing world.

1. *The Challenge of Spiritual Renewal*

How well do our churches now fulfil their mission as the people of God? At the moment when American churches are achieving their most notable institutional success, many prophetic voices are being raised to question the effectiveness of their witness for Christ. Even now, books rush from the press to diagnose the ills of the Christian community. These writings emphasize, mainly, that too many churches are more oriented to an American "religion in general" than they are to the redemptive life of men in Christ. We are warned that, unless the tendency to a comfortable institutionalism is reversed, churches are destined to be less and less usable to the redemptive purposes of God. God may bypass us as he fulfils his goal in history. Some among us express a similar concern for Christian witness and plead for spiritual renewal in the church. See, for example, Findley B. Edge, *A Quest for Vitality in Religion.*

It seems increasingly difficult for Southern Baptists to win the "outsider's" hearing of the gospel. As with all American churches, unbelievers are not attending our churches as they once did. Evangelistic meetings rarely reach large numbers of the unsaved. By and large, we do not reach the masses we once reached with the gospel. Nor do we reach many in the higher intellectual and executive circles, although both groups desperately need the gospel.

Sermons have not lost their evangelistic appeal, as some believe, so much as they have been addressed to people who are not present to hear them. The tragedy of many pulpits is that ministers speak to those not present in language that they would not understand if they were present. Thus, the pulpit speaks dynamically to no one.

The lost provinces of the church's witness also disturb us. Many churches continue to exert a strong influence for the Christian way of life in their communities. Yet, it must be admitted that most churches seem to make less and less difference in our secularistic and revolutionary age.

A lecturer spoke recently at Yale University on the subject of preaching. He lamented this lost dynamic. He said that good evidence of the declining significance of our witness exists in the appearance of "News of the Churches" newspaper columns on Saturday rather than Monday. "The news is that the church *is* to assemble, not that it *has* assembled." [1] It ought to make a great deal of difference that Southern Baptist churches meet every Sunday for worship. All too often, however, the church is more molded by the world than it molds a world for Christ. At least there seems to be little of the "turning of the world upside down" which marked the impact of the first century church.

There is a need for spiritual renewal within our churches. The presence of such excesses as the modern *glossolalia* (tongues) movement, to which some Baptists and many other evangelical Christians are drawn, may well reflect the spiritual void in much that we do in our churches. We need a renewal of commitment to the lordship of Christ. Then, honest critics can no longer say, "We Christians . . . make our daily decisions and judgments about people, events, and

---

[1] Browne Barr, *Parish Back Talk* (New York: Abingdon Press, 1964), p. 83.

ourselves largely by standards borrowed from and shared with the society about us." [2]

Spiritual renewal will result in the church's actual presence *in* the world, to love and to lose themselves in the redemptive purposes of Christ. One of the great challenges to Southern Baptists is so genuine a recovery of their redemptive mission that their churches will live in the world in the spirit of incarnation and crucifixion, that the "mind of Christ" may be reflected in their witness.

2. *The Challenge of an Urban Culture*

The world in which churches today proclaim the gospel is a new kind of world. One of the distinctive marks of the American scene is the change from a rural to an urban culture.

A nation that was 90 per cent rural at the turn of the Eighteenth Century has become, by 1960, approximately 65 per cent urban. Large cities multiply in America. If the present trend continues, over ⅔ of our population will reside in metropolitan areas by 1975.[3] Accompanying the growth of large cities, suburban population has greatly increased in the last decades. The current trend is toward the development of the megalopolis—the extension and virtual joining of several large cities in an area to form a huge metropolitan population. By the turn of the century America will be dotted by these extended cities.

The urbanizing of America is more than the growth of large cities, however. It is the development of a basic way of life. Industrialization, big business, science and technology, mass communications, the arts, changes in education, the mobility

[2] Langdon Gilkey, *How the Church Can Minister to the World Without Losing Itself* (New York: Harper & Row, 1964), p. 21.

[3] Gibson Winter, *The Suburban Captivity of the Churches* (Garden City, New York: Doubleday & Co., Inc., 1961), p. 16.

of the population (one million Americans move their residence every year), rapid transportation, the increase of leisure time—these are marks of America's new way of life.

Southern Baptists, once a people of rural and provincial cultural background, now confront an almost total urban culture. Not only have we gone to the big city, as churches have been established in areas outside the South, but the city has come to us in an industrialized and rapidly changing South. We confront such dilemmas as: How can we witness in the inner city, where we, like most Protestants, have tended to "pack up" our churches and to move them with our furniture to suburbia, or else to stay in the inner-city but to draw membership totally from areas other than the church's locale? How can we witness in high-rise apartment areas, as the suburban trend turns back to city living; how to witness in the urban culture where many races and economic levels live close together and where the church and the "sponsored mission" concept may have lost its power to reach men for Christ? How can we witness to and win to Christ people who are native residents of an area, rather than building churches completely upon "transplanted" Baptists from the South? How can we witness in an age of leisure? The challenge multiplies.

3. *The Challenge of an Exploding Population*

Proclamation must be increased in a world that literally explodes in its population growth. The United Nations has predicted that four billion people will live on our planet by 1975 and that, if the present birthrate continues, the world population will soon number 7 billion. The same figures indicate that the population of the United States will increase to 450 million in this century.[4]

---

[4] Roy L. Smith, *The Future Is Upon Us* (New York: Abingdon Press, 1962), p. 19.

This growth not only creates problems of food, space for living, education, welfare, and government. It also creates a challenge for Christian proclamation. Far more people are born into the world in any year than all Christian groups combined are winning to Christ. We are rapidly losing the world, population-wise, for Christianity. Paul's lament is relevant: "How shall they believe in him of whom they have not heard? and how shall they hear without a preacher?" (Rom. 10:14). When these and other challenges of our time are considered, the Christian mission of witness becomes urgent indeed.

II. WITNESS—EVERY CHRISTIAN'S VOCATION

Doubtless in our kind of world, in which the church's proclamation of the gospel faces the competition and complexities of a new age, new and creative forms of witness are needed. Existing organizations and methods need reexamination. But of great importance to Christian advance in the world is the reclaiming of personal witness as every Christian's vocation.

Every Christian shares in the Christian calling. For all of us, it is a calling to salvation, to the lordship of Christ, and to righteous living. But we all share also in the calling to participate in God's redemptive work among men. God's call to the ministry is not distinguished at the point of Christian witness. Rather, as one theologian expresses it, "The church does not have a mission, but the Church is a mission, and it is performed by all members with their gifts of grace, which are given for the edification of the Church and the service to the unbelievers." [5] If the church is to go into the world, it must go through every member as he proclaims Christ, whatever his work may be.

---

[5] Dietrich Ritschl, *A Theology of Proclamation* (Richmond: John Knox Press, 1960), p. 117.

1. *The Biblical Evidence for a Common Ministry of Personal Witness*

The truth that every Christian shares in the ministry of witness finds eloquent statement in Ephesians 4:7–16. Paul is discussing the various gifts which Christ bestows upon the church. He writes, "And he gave some, apostles; and some, prophets; and some, evangelists; and some, pastors and teachers; for the perfecting of the saints, for the work of the ministry, for the edifying of the body of Christ" (vv. 11–12). English versions of this passage, by the insertion of commas after each phrase in verse 12, make it refer to three functions of pastors and other specially appointed ministers. These functions are: to perfect the saints, to do the work of the ministry, and to build up the body of Christ.

Actually, however, Paul changes prepositions in this verse and thus gives it a revolutionary meaning. He affirms, most New Testament scholars contend, that the work of the pastor and other specially-called ministers in God's economy for the church is to perfect the "saints" that they may do the work of the ministry, so that the entire church may become a "full grown man." [6]

Christ, then, has given every Christian the responsibility to witness. This does not mean that there is no unique call to the gospel ministry, but it means that every man so divinely called "is the minister of a ministering community. He is a preacher to other preachers." [7]

---

[6] See Dale Moody, *Christ and the Church* (Grand Rapids: Wm. B. Eerdmans Publishing Co., 1963), p. 94; Francis Foulkes, *The Epistle of Paul to the Ephesians*, "The Tyndale New Testament Commentaries," R. V. G. Tasker, ed., (Grand Rapids: Wm. B. Eerdmans Publishing Co., 1963), p. 120; Ray Summers, *Ephesians: Pattern for Christian Living* (Nashville: Broadman Press, 1960), pp. 85–86.

[7] Roy Pearson, *The Preacher: His Purpose and Practice* (Philadelphia: The Westminster Press, 1962), p. 85.

The New Testament abounds with examples of personal witness to the gospel. Andrew bore witness to his personal discovery of the Christ (John 1:40–42). The Gadarene demoniac declared how "great things Jesus had done for him" (Mark 5:20). The blind man spoke of the certainty of his experience with Jesus of Nazareth (John 9:25). Philip "preached" to the Ethiopian in the explanation and invitation of personal witness (Acts 8:26f). The biblical evidence substantiates Elton Trueblood's claim: "A person cannot be a Christian and avoid being an evangelist." [8]

2. *The Vocation of Verbal Witness*

Many Christians avoid a personal witness to the unsaved on the grounds that they, although timid to speak to persons about Christ, seek to "live their religion." While witness through life is paramount to proclamation, every Christian is to bear verbal testimony to the gospel. He should bear witness to the facts of God's redemptive act in Christ and to its meaning in his own life.

Such personal witness to unbelievers must be tactfully done so as not to violate personal freedom or the Holy Spirit's work in converting men to Christ. But it is impossible to understand that one who has known the reality of encounter with Christ should remain silent about the "good news" of "his" gospel. Peter said of Christians, "We cannot but speak the things that we have seen and heard" (Acts 4:20).

3. *The Vocation of Living Witness*

No Christian may escape his responsibility to be a verbal witness. However, the quality of a life that is "in Christ" remains the primary communication with the world. It is by the Christian living of its members that a church reaches the

---

[8] Elton Trueblood, *The Company of the Committed* (New York: Harper & Bros., 1961), p. 55.

world. Christ should be proclaimed in redeemed relationships marked by love and forgiveness in every person-to-person encounter: in the home, in the social world, in daily work. Without the witness of life, verbal witness is void. Just at this point, the need for renewal in our churches becomes glaringly apparent.

The division of life into the sacred and the secular, that leaves many church members content with a fragmented and "Sunday only" religion, must go. Findley Edge states the case well: "Unless the gospel becomes incarnate in the lives of church members, 'the world' will never see or hear. It is quite probable that this incarnate witness must be given to the world before the world will ever listen or be able to understand a verbal witness." [9]

It is through his personal witnessing that the Christian bears dynamic proclamation of Jesus. The priesthood of every believer asserts that he not only may come to God for himself in Christ, but he may live all of life for God as a participant in his work of redemption. The practice of this doctrine would result in the greatest outreach for Christ our churches have ever known. Planned programs of visitation, good as far as they go, would give way to daily witness in the world. After all, the church is already in the world when its members leave the assembly of worship. The church lives in apartments, works in the factories, and studies on the campuses.

Why should the church not penetrate all of the world with the gospel witness? Pastors would suddenly have as many "assistants" as they have members. Such a multiple ministry would enhance the pastors' own witness and would afford them greater opportunity to preach effectively. Thus they could equip other Christians for their ministry in the world. Above all, the practice of the priesthood of every believer

---

[9] *A Quest for Vitality in Religion* (Nashville: Broadman Press, 1963), pp. 140–41.

would recover the biblical image of the church, not as a place to go, but as "the company of the committed" at work in the world. It would eliminate "spectator Christianity," and it would engage all Christians in their true vocation as followers of Christ.

III. Accomplishing the Christian Vocation of Witness

The participation of every Christian in proclamation through witness in word and deed will not be realized without effort. Our failure in proclamation makes it clear that much we are doing must be done better. Also, we must take bold new ventures in Christian discipleship. The following suggestions, all briefly stated, are worthy of consideration.

1. *A Greater Concern for a Redeemed Church Membership*

Christian discipleship must be understood for what it is—the commitment of all of life to the lordship of Christ. We cannot have witnesses for Christ until men know Christ.

Preachers and teachers must declare the demands of the gospel clearly and forcefully. Appeals for decision for Christ must be directed to the will of man. Care must be taken to explain the meaning of repentance and faith. The clarion call of Christ "Come, take up the cross and follow me" must never be compromised. Evangelism must be made more and more biblical in scope and depth. We have thought too little about the baptism of young children into the church without careful counseling, with the result that many adults have an unhappy and fruitless Christian relationship. All who present themselves for church membership should be dealt with personally to determine their understanding of the experience. In short, every Christian's ministry as a witness for Christ depends, first of all, upon a redemptive experience. Having cherished this tenet of the faith, Baptists must now practice its discipline more earnestly.

2. *A Recovery of the Personal*

Closely related to this is the need for greater concern for persons in our churches. In a program-centered church life, the worth of the person can be easily lost. Greater compassion is a gift which only the Holy Spirit can give. This compassion will lead to person-centered evangelism, to a person-centered ministry to Christians, and to the involvement of every person, in his own way and place, in the vocation of witness for his Lord.

3. *A More Effective Training Ministry*

Our people need instruction in the Christian life. The many opportunities for instruction already in our churches should be utilized more fully. The contribution of the pulpit, for example, to the instruction and inspiration for personal witness can be of inestimatable worth. Sunday school classes, Training Union groups—in fact, every existing organization for the teaching of the Bible and Christian discipleship should be more fully used.

But we must enlarge our existing program in equipping church members for Christian witness. Much more must be done in Bible study than is possible in the brief time allotted on Sunday. There is no reason why laymen should not become acquainted with theology and Christian philosophy. Such training would better equip every Christian to bear witness to his faith intelligently and convincingly. The Training Union is the church organization given this responsibility.

Potential for training in depth can be found in small fellowship groups. These groups afford splendid opportunities for Bible study, the deepening of prayer life, and the discussion of current theological and ethical issues of concern for Christian proclamation. In this close fellowship, new avenues for Christian witness, such as the penetration of all vocations, can be explored.

4. *New Opportunities for Ministry*

No amount of training will be of use unless adequate opportunity is given for every Christian to participate in proclamation. Churches should provide their members with the privileges of care for persons, which belong to every Christian. The program of the spiritual ministry of deacons, which many churches utilize, is a good start. The metropolitan church, particularly in the inner-city, can well engage in new ministries for the families about its doors. This would afford through its members concern for the total person demonstrated in the witness of Jesus.

Increasingly, Baptists need to afford opportunity and encouragement for the Christian's witness in his home and community. More use of church members in the worship services of the church will inspire their witness.

We live in a new world. Its loss of concern for God alarms us. Its rapid rate of living and travel exhausts our imagination. Its space-age knowledge threatens self-destruction on the one hand and promises an age of unbelievable scientific achievement on the other. This poses the most urgent task for proclamation Christians have ever faced. In such a time, business-as-usual in our churches will not do. All who call themselves Christians must be committed to Christ and trained in proclamation. Then, they must boldly carry the Saviour and his redemptive message to the world.

FOR STUDY AND CLASS DISCUSSION

FOR FURTHER STUDY

1. Study the personal interviews of Jesus. What lessons for personal witness can be learned from them?

2. Make a study of the New Testament's teaching on the Christian callings. Why do Baptists believe in a unique call to the

ministry? What is distinctive about such a call? What callings do all Christians share in common?

3. Research the many study course books available in your library on the subject of personal witness. Compile a list of suggestions for a more effective personal witness to the unsaved.

FOR DISCUSSION AND CLASSWORK

1. In what ways has the urbanization of the American culture affected your church and its proclamation of the gospel?

2. Discuss some of the values of small fellowship groups for the strengthening of personal witness.

3. What are some of the vocations and other areas of our modern culture that have special needs for the gospel? Make some suggestions as to more effective proclamation in these areas.

4. What could your church do to afford church members more opportunities and encouragement for personal witnessing?

CHAPTER 7

7

That by All Means
We May Win Some

ONE IMPORTANT DISCOVERY of this study has been that a biblical theology of proclamation permits many forms of witness to the gospel. To this point, we have stated that preaching must remain primary to Christian proclamation. Indeed, the effectiveness of every other means of witness depends on the effectiveness of the pulpit.

In chapter 6, however, we emphasized that the Christian church goes into the world through the personal witness, both in word and deed, of every Christian. The concept of church members supporting their pastor so that he can proclaim the gospel for them is not biblical. Rather, New Testament discipleship involves every believer in a redemptive mission. The pastor supports his members so that they can join him in their common vocation of witness.

There yet remain other means by which the gospel can be proclaimed. In this chapter, we shall mention several such forms of Christian witness.

I. PROCLAMATION THROUGH WORSHIP

Christian proclamation occurs in worship. This does not simply repeat the emphasis that preaching, central to worship, is proclamation. It means, as stated in the first chapter, that the proclamation of the gospel occurs in many acts of

109

public worship and that by the congregation's assembly in response to God's grace in worship, they corporately proclaim the gospel to the world.

Proclamation occurs in the reading of the Scriptures. In this moment, if the Scriptures are read well and understandably, God's Word becomes clearer than at any other time. For this reason, ministers and other worship leaders should read the Bible aloud with effectiveness. The time when the Scriptures are read should become a meaningful part of worship, and the congregation, by varying means, should participate in the reading. Proclamation through the reading of the Scriptures may be less effective if the only biblical text used in a worship service is the minister's short sermon text.

Christians proclaim the gospel through music also. Congregational singing is worship by reason of man's response to God in praise. But it also affords every participant a means of proclaiming his faith in Christ to others. Proclamation may be found in the use of anthems, solos, and other special music. Thus, the worth of music to worship as proclamation and response makes its choice a matter of theological responsibility.

Baptism and the Lord's Supper are means of gospel witness. When believers are baptized, they proclaim the death and resurrection of Christ pictorally. They also bear witness to their own spiritual resurrection from death to walk in "newness of life" (Rom. 6:4). The observance of the Supper also gives witness to God's redemptive act in Christ. Baptists should observe the ordinances with greater care, with more understanding of their meaning, and in deeper reverence. Though the ordinances are symbols, they are dynamic symbols with profound significance for worship and proclamation.

When the congregation assembles to worship, they bear corporate witness to the world that God alone is Lord of heaven and earth. Before the people of God can be the church dispersed in proclamation, they must be the church gathered for proclamation of the gospel and for an ever deepening communion with God. By better worship, Southern Baptists will become better witnesses of the gospel.

II. PROCLAMATION THROUGH MISSIONS

The church proclaims through missions. Some are commissioned by the Holy Spirit to bear witness to Christ in areas of spiritual darkness through special ministries. Southern Baptists need to make a new effort to "call out the called" for missions from among the most capable youth of the churches. Support for missions, foreign and home, must continue and increase. But added to this, in a rapidly decreasing world in terms of transportation and communication, bold new ventures in missions need to be made.

The place to begin is with an interpretation of missions as every Christian's responsibility, reaching from Main Street to the farthest nation. The principle of personal witness described in the last chapter should be applied to missions. If every Christian in the military, in business, and in travel were to proclaim Christ by word and deed wherever he is in the world, our missionary forces would be magnificently multiplied.

We must also learn that effective proclamation of the gospel in today's world requires more than sermons and dollars, as significant as they are. But is this new? The incarnation of Jesus preceded his preaching. The same principle must be true with his people today in their witness. Proclamation in missions is weakened when we have an "easy" concern for people with a foreign address, but lack a genuine compassion for the same kind of people at our doorsteps.

On the other hand, a concentration on the local institutional church, to the neglect of a lost world, defames any people's claim to be missionary. Baptists need to become more aware of the world, of its peoples and their hurts, and of the meaning of the events of its history. And, then, they need to get personally involved in the costly price of the gospel's witness in our time. We must not resist the examination of any mission methods that will result in a more biblical and effective communication with the world.

III. PROCLAMATION THROUGH TEACHING

Biblical proclamation is sufficiently broad in scope to include instruction in the Christian life. Thus, the teaching of inquirers or of converts in preparation for baptism or for growth in the Christian faith and life becomes a means of Christian witness.

Counseling sessions are of special redemptive significance, especially for children. Conversion is a definite experience in point of time and not a process of education. Yet, these classes are designed to interpret the nature of the conversion experience and the mission of the Christian life and community. Such training, definitely of the nature of proclamation, will make for genuine decisions for Christ later.

The new Christian needs training in the nature of the gospel he has received. Consider one phase of this need that has not been discussed previously. Recently, a letter from a disturbed mother came to my desk. She was asking for help for her son, whose faith in God was shaken by a university professor's skepticism. The letter, like many similar ones, points up a need for our churches to train their youth more effectively in the nature of the biblical revelation, the doctrines of our faith, the meaning of the Christian vocation, and the significance of commitment to Christ.

We Southern Baptists have more than our share of young people whose Christian commitments are unexamined and who become casualties to the intellectual, social, and moral pressures of campus life. We must go deeper into their Christian training. Such training will add stability to young Christian personalities, and it will be one of the church's best means of dialogue with the campus world, where her province of influence was once strong.

Finally, as in proclamation to unbelievers, the responsibility for teaching does not reside in the minister alone. All Christians share in Christ's commission to teach the nations (Matt. 28:19-20). Every Christian is to use his "gift," which in many cases is a talent for instruction, to bring the church to spiritual maturity (Eph. 4:7-16).

IV. PROCLAMATION THROUGH SOCIAL AND MORAL CONCERN

The people of God cannot escape their responsibility to contend for civic righteousness. The vocation of church members to bear Christian witness is the prime means of such proclamation. Redeemed men continue to be the hope of a redeemed society. Committed Christians need to be encouraged to take more active participation in politics, government, and school and civil leadership. Then, their witness for Christ can become more effective for moral and social righteousness.

The proclamation of the ethical implications of the gospel also must assume other forms. The Christian pulpit not only has a biblical right, but also a biblical responsibility, to speak for God on all matters pertaining to God's redemptive mission in the world. More biblical- and redemption-centered sermons need to be preached on controversial issues. Our Baptist people need to develop a conscience on the "mind of Christ" about the burning issues of our time.

This is another one of those places where the cost of Christian discipleship is higher than a comfortable, institutional success image. The scene of a complacent and silent church against the backdrop of a world flaming with crises is not a pleasant one. If our churches are not involved in the proclamation of God's Word to every issue of gospel concern, they render themselves useless at that point to God's purposes in history.

V. Proclamation Through Pastoral Care

Pastoral care, like preaching, proceeds from the Word of God, and it is redemptive in content and purpose. As Eduard Thurneysen writes, pastoral care is a "special discourse" distinguished from profane and natural speech and designed for the care of the soul of man.[1] Christ speaks through such conversation to redeem men from the darknes of turmoil and spiritual distress.

Every Christian has a ministry of proclamation through "pastoral concern." But the responsibility for the development of this concern in every member of the church rests first with the pastor. He must shepherd his people. It is he who most effectively proclaims God's forgiveness and healing for the hurts of his people. To do so, pastors must be concerned about persons. A wise Christian attorney, addressing a group of pastors, reminded them of their impatience with the interests and problems of their people. He said, "If you would learn to listen more, some of us who are lawyers and doctors would not have to listen so much."

The minister must lead his church to be a community of reconciliation. Thus, they could proclaim to the world the powers of redemptive fellowship. The minister must set the pace for a spiritual community where compassion holds the primacy. This would be a community more interested in persons than in material and statistical success. By so doing, the pastor truly becomes a minister to ministers. He is used of God in the growth of Christian persons, and the entire church would become the servants of proclamation.

VI. Proclamation Through the Mass Media

The mass media of communication, especially radio and television, offer to Baptists and all other Christians increas-

---

[1] *A Theology of Pastoral Care,* trans. by Jack A. Worthington and Thomas Wieser (Richmond: John Knox Press, 1962), pp. 101–14.

ing opportunities for the proclamation of the gospel. Communication satellites now afford global television. They offer the future potential of direct communication with home television receivers without benefit of station outlet. This medium offers tremendous mission potential for preaching the gospel in countries where missions are impossible or limited.

The Southern Baptist Radio and Television Commission continues to make many creative contributions to proclamation through the mass media. In addition to their work, Baptist colleges and seminaries should provide adequate training in the use of radio and television. More and more, local churches can take advantage of these outlets for the communication of the gospel—not merely by the broadcast of worship services, but by new dimensions of religious programing as well.

VII. Proclamation Through Religious Drama and Other Art Forms

The art forms have great witness potential that should be increasingly appreciated and used by Baptists. On a recent Easter Sunday, a large Southern Baptist church in Florida gave the two morning services to the presentation of the gospel of the resurrection through drama. Occasional use of forms other than the traditional sermon will make effective our proclamation. Music and art also may reach some yet unreached by other means of witness.

VIII. Proclamation Through New Forms of the Church's Witness

In the last chapter, we confronted the difficulty which Southern Baptists face in bearing effective witness for Christ in the large metropolitan areas of the nation. Often, the organizational structure which has succeeded in the South does not seem to be effective in the large urban centers where Southern Baptists' greatest evangelistic opportunity now exists. We need new and creative forms of witness as we think of such challenges as high-rise apartments, shorter work weeks, and the peculiar patterns and pressures of life in the big city.

We must recover from our fixation that God is not concerned with the city. We can learn from the experiments in metropolitan witness and ministry which have been made by such groups as the Church of the Saviour in Washington and the East Harlem Protestant Mission in New York. These ministries include such unorthodox approaches as coffee houses. Some of the most fruitful missionary fields of the world are in the vast population centers of America, where Southern Baptists now attempt a creative ministry. Since so much of our future is in these areas, we can be grateful for the study of metropolitan evangelism now being conducted by the Evangelism Department of the Home Mission Board and by some of our seminaries.

Many other means of witness to the gospel could be listed in this study. For example, we have not discussed the value of writing, an important communication potential. This will be sufficient, however, to demonstrate the wide scope of Christian proclamation which challenges the contemporary Christian. By whatever means dialogue can be established with the people of our world, the gospel can and should be proclaimed. Preaching is the climactic act of proclamation in the climactic hour of proclamation, the hour of the church's assembled worship. From this act and hour, the church should, through every Christian, emerge to make use of all legitimate media of witness to Christ, that by all means we may win some to our Lord and Saviour.

FOR STUDY AND CLASS DISCUSSION

FOR FURTHER STUDY

This chapter has only suggested the many means by which the gospel can be proclaimed effectively. How many other means of presenting the redemptive claims of Christ to the world today can you describe?

FOR DISCUSSION AND CLASSWORK

1. Have several members of the class select a creative means of witness. Discuss it thoroughly as to value and specific suggestions for effective use.

2. Discuss and evaluate, in light of the biblical material and our contemporary world, Southern Baptist mission methods.

3. What do you feel is the proper role of the church and pulpit in matters of moral and social concern?

CHAPTER 8

8

Dynamic for the Task

THE MORE DEMANDING THE TASK, the greater the power that is required to perform it. Since proclamation participates in redemptive history, only the power of the Holy Spirit can make proclamation effective.

Neither the sermon, personal witness, nor any other form of proclamation can be spiritually powerful without the dynamic of the Holy Spirit. Neither churches, ministers, nor Christian laymen can achieve what has been defined as proclamation without the Holy Spirit's presence and power.

No one ever recognized proclamation's dependence on God's Spirit more than Paul. In describing the nature of his ministry at Corinth, he writes, "I was with you in weakness and in much fear and trembling; and my speech and my message were not in plausible words of wisdom, but in demonstration of the Spirit and power, that your faith might not rest in the wisdom of men but in the power of God" (1 Cor. 2:3-5, RSV).

Paul meant no reflection on true wisdom. He simply admitted, in contrast to the proud spirit of the Corinthians, that the best of man's knowledge and strength are not enough for the redemptive work of God's people. Paul placed no confidence in the excellence of worldly speech and wisdom. He trembled at his own inability. He rested the case of proclamation on the Spirit and power of God.

It is appropriate to end this study of proclamation and witness with an emphasis on the dynamic needed for their effectiveness. We shall observe three brief facts about the Holy Spirit as the dynamic for the Christian vocation of witness.

I. THE HOLY SPIRIT—A PROMISE FULFILLED

Henry P. Van Dusen, in his excellent book *Spirit, Son and Father*, states that everywhere in the Bible the Spirit of God is the intimacy and potency of God. He is God's activity and God's presence, making possible a personal religion.[1] In the Old Testament, the Holy Spirit is pictured as God's creative activity. The Spirit came upon men, calling and empowering them for their tasks. Such visitations were occasional, however.

Accompanying the occasional empowering of the Holy Spirit in the Old Testament, there were promises of a new dimension for his future ministry. Isaiah prophesied, "I will pour my spirit upon thy seed, and my blessing upon thine offspring" (Isa. 44:3). Joel voiced the same hope, "I will pour out my Spirit upon all flesh" (Joel 2:28).

Then, Jesus Christ came into the world. He was born, guided, and empowered for life, death, and the resurrection by God's Spirit. From his lips came a dramatic renewal of the promise: "And I will pray the Father, and he will give you another Counselor, to be with you for ever, even the Spirit of truth" (John 14:16-17, RSV). After his resurrection, Jesus stood with his disciples on the threshold of their mission to urge them "to wait for the promise of the Father, which, he said, 'you heard from me, for John baptized with water, but before many days you shall be baptized with the Holy Spirit'" (Acts 1:4-5, RSV). He promised them power to be his "witnesses in Jerusalem and in all Judea and Samaria and to the end of the earth" (Acts 1:8, RSV).

They waited! And on the day of Pentecost, God kept his

---

[1] New York: Charles Scribner's Sons, 1958, pp. 17f.

promise. The Holy Spirit fell upon them, not as an occasional visitation, but as an indwelling presence in the believer's heart. Ordinary men were transformed. Their powers were heightened. They proclaimed the living Christ with power, they did many of the "signs and wonders" which had marked the ministry of Jesus. And they marched out to conquer an unbelieving world for Christ.

The promise of God has been kept. The Spirit of God abides with his people to equip them for their mission in the world. And wherever they have been vital and dynamic, the Spirit has been at the heart of their Christian experience and proclamation.[2]

II. THE HOLY SPIRIT—A POWER NEGLECTED

A close identity between vital proclamation and the Spirit of God exists. It seems logical to associate inadequate Christian witness with the neglect of the Holy Spirit. Indeed, there is abundant evidence that the renewal of proclamation in our time depends primarily upon a revival of an awareness of and a dependence upon the Spirit of God.

All too often, men attempt to proclaim Christ without a reliance upon God's power. Conviction and conversion are the work of the Holy Spirit. A vast difference exists between Christianity as a teaching and Christianity as a personal experience. Men may be persuaded to accept ideas by oratory and logic. People may be drawn down aisles and into churches by methods of mass psychology. But only the Holy Spirit can make Christianity into a personal experience. Only God's Spirit can confront men with Christ and give them new life in him. The Holy Spirit alone convicts of sin. Jesus said, "And when he is come, he will reprove the world of sin, and of righteousness, and of judgment" (John 16:8). The Holy Spirit alone invites men to come to Christ and empowers

---

[2] *Ibid.*, p. 126.

them to commit themselves to him (John 6:44; 1 Cor. 12:3).

No proclaimer of the gospel has the right, then, to take the Holy Spirit's place in bringing men to Christ. It is the proclaimer's task to bear witness to the gospel and to invite men to respond to it. It is God's task to win man's ultimate decision. A searching question every church needs to face as they examine their ministry of proclamation is, What are we doing that could not be done without the power of God?

We often rely for the effectiveness of our communication upon the methods of an institutional religion much more than upon the one dynamic necessary to spiritual power. Samuel Shoemaker said, "What the Church truly needs is the Holy Spirit, deep fellowship at the center of its life, and witness in life and words as its overflow." [3]

Another indication of a neglect of the Holy Spirit is the silence of our witness. One of the evidences of spiritual renewal at Pentecost was that timid men began to speak the Word of God with a holy boldness. After the Spirit of God fell upon them, they began to witness everywhere. In houses and temples, in synagogues and council chambers, in jails and on the decks of ships—they proclaimed Christ.

In contrast, much of modern Christianity bears a muffled witness to Christ. Great masses of Christians are never seized by the urgency of their responsibility to proclaim Christ in word and deed. The modern church's preoccupation with its institutional success, its status, and its security has all too often hushed a witness for Christ. Losing the power to be different, we have frequently acquiesced to our culture and have lost our power to proclaim Christ to our world.

Thus, many times the world is unmoved by the witness we bear. In contrast, at Pentecost the world reacted with a knowledge that something dynamic had happened. G. Campbell Morgan pictures the reaction as one of amazement, per-

[3] Samuel Shoemaker, *With the Holy Spirit and with Fire* (New York: Harper & Bros., 1960), p. 96.

plexity, and criticism.[4] The early Christians were often criticized, opposed, rejected, and killed. But one thing is certain—the world did not ignore them.

When proclamation occurs in the power of the Holy Spirit, the world must react. Christ's witnesses have no modern promise of being accepted by the world. But when God truly speaks through his people in the power of his Spirit, they will not be ignored easily. What shall we say then of the "toleration" which the modern church receives from the world? How shall we analyze the all too frequent ineffectiveness of our witness? Perhaps he has the answer who writes, "Slowly but surely today . . . God is driving the church into a corner from which there is no escape . . . God is stripping from us every false hope and making us face reality. He is teaching us these days that nothing less than the outpouring of the Holy Spirit in revival can ever meet the need."[5]

III. THE HOLY SPIRIT—A PEOPLE POSSESSED BY POWER

The source of divine power and proclamation's need for it are apparent. The question remains: How shall we experience the renewal of the presence of the Holy Spirit in our Christian witness? The answer finds eloquent expression in the writing of Paul to the Corinthians quoted at the beginning of this chapter.

The message we proclaim determines our usefulness to the Spirit of God. The message Paul preached was "Christ and him crucified." Throughout this study, the central importance of gospel content for proclamation has been emphasized. All that we have previously discussed, then, concerning *kerygmatic* and biblical proclamation is of importance here. God has chosen to speak through man, but only when man's

[4] G. Campbell Morgan, *The Acts of the Apostles* (New York: Fleming H. Revell Co., 1924), p. 38.

[5] Alan Redpath, *The Royal Route to Heaven* (Westwood, New Jersey: Fleming H. Revell Co., 1960), pp. 35–36.

proclamation is the Word of God. If we are to know the power of the Holy Spirit upon our witness, we must, by word and deed, be servants of the Word of God.

Our power also depends upon our complete reliance upon the Spirit of God for the effectiveness of our proclamation and witness. Paul "trembled at himself." Facing the challenge at Corinth, he, who of all men might have relied upon himself, spoke of being with them "in weakness and fear." He placed no confidence in himself. He took no side glances at his own success. Instead, he emptied himself of self. His was no false humility which degraded self. But it was a recognition that apart from God he was powerless.

Our power depends upon our full dedication to Christ. This is the positive side of humility. Paul "trembled" at himself and "decided" to empty himself of every other knowledge except Jesus Christ. This speaks of more than a message. This speaks of a life commitment. The Spirit of God cannot use a proud, self-reliant people. The way to renewal of power in proclamation is the way of self-sacrifice and full commitment to Christ.

Such commitment was the power of Pentecost. As the disciples waited in prayer, their minds were full of Christ. And, then, he came! His living presence filled them with an unspeakable power for their mission in the world. So it must be with us. We must so commit ourselves to Christ that we are ready to follow him, bearing a cross, speaking his word whatever the price or place. Christ must be Lord of the church and of our lives. If our proclamation is to be with power, we must be caught up out of our petty orbits of concern into the eternal purposes of God in Christ.

We need no new Pentecost. For since that significant day in redemptive history, the Spirit of God has been present among his people in the heart of every believer. But we desperately need a new filling of his power that we may witness effectively. Let us be certain of our message. Let us be dedicated to God's redemptive purposes. Let us so commit ourselves to Christ that we will be concerned with his concern and involved with his involvement in the world. Then, with love, let us speak in word and life for him. His Spirit will then be our power.

FOR STUDY AND CLASS DISCUSSION

FOR FURTHER STUDY

At this time, there is widespread interest in a renewal of the ministry of the Holy Spirit. The modern tongues movement is one expression of this interest. Examine the tongues movement in light of the biblical doctrine of the Holy Spirit. What are its excesses? What message does it speak to our contemporary church life? You can find an excellent discussion and fuller bibliography for this study in an article by John Newport in his book *The Holy Spirit Empowers Christian Workers*.

FOR DISCUSSION AND CLASSWORK

Do current emphases indicate a desire for spiritual renewal among church members? What evidences of the need of spiritual power do you feel exist in Christian proclamation? Do you detect evidences of spiritual revival in proclamation in our time?

FOR REVIEW AND WRITTEN WORK

CHAPTER 1

1. What is Christian proclamation?
2. What evidences have you found in your experience and in your church that there is a need for a study of proclamation?
3. In what ways should Christians and churches seek to penetrate the modern world?
4. What are the theological demands for proclamation?

CHAPTER 2

5. Why is it correct to say that the Old Testament contains preparation for proclamation rather than proclamation itself?
6. How are the Old Testament prophets important for a study of Christian proclamation?
7. What are the two terms which are always used in the New Testament to refer to witness to the unsaved?
8. What was the essential content of apostolic proclamation?
9. How are preaching and teaching related in the New Testament?
10. What evidence can be found in the New Testament that instruction in the Christian life properly can be termed proclamation?

CHAPTER 3

11. Name some of the themes of New Testament proclamation.
12. Why is Peter's sermon at Pentecost of such vital importance for an understanding of New Testament proclamation?
13. What makes Peter's sermon to Cornelius and Paul's sermon on Mars' Hill important for Christian proclamation?
14. What points of emphasis do the recorded sermons of the New Testament have in common?

CHAPTER 4

15. What does the term "redemptive history" mean to you?
16. What is the significance of the life of Jesus for redemption?

17. What demands does the cross of Jesus make upon men?
18. In what way can we speak of salvation as past, present, and future?

CHAPTER 5

19. What changes in your attitude toward the nature and importance of preaching have you experienced as a result of this study?
20. Why is preaching primary in Christian proclamation?
21. Why is it true that preaching participates in redemptive history?
22. What kind of preaching qualifies as Christian proclamation?

CHAPTER 6

23. Why does your church's maximum effectiveness in the proclamation of the gospel depend on personal witnessing by every one of its members?
24. What are some New Testament evidences that every Christian has a ministry of personal witness?
25. What do we mean by the doctrine of the priesthood of the believer?
26. Why is witness of life essential to Christian proclamation?
27. How can Southern Baptists more successfully involve all church members in their vocation of witness?

CHAPTER 7

28. Name several ways, other than preaching and personal witness, by which the gospel can be proclaimed.
29. Suggest some unusual ways in which your church has proclaimed the gospel in the last year.

CHAPTER 8

30. Why must Christian proclamation depend on the Holy Spirit for its effectiveness?
31. How can Christian proclamation and witness in our time be empowered by the Holy Spirit?

TEACHING HELPS

T. GARVICE MURPHREE

PREPARATION

Read the entire book as early as possible. Then make a deeper, more careful study by chapters and topics.

It may be helpful to remember that there has been a continuing debate among some theologians as to the relative places of preaching and teaching. You will realize early that this is a book on theology—the theology of proclamation.

Two objectives are recommended for your consideration; first, be receptive to new means of proclamation; second, try to lead each class member to become personally involved in proclamation.

Three suggestions are made as guiding principles in the teaching procedure:

1. Remember that learning is more likely to occur when the teacher thinks of pupils as participants in learning efforts.

2. Plan and conduct each session around *one* important idea.

3. Remember that visual images are essential for fixing ideas readily in the minds of pupils.

In the light of these principles, extensive use should be made of key words, symbols, illustrations, and drawings. Even when prepared by nonprofessionals, such aids can be very effective.

Discussion (in varying degrees of formality), lecture, study-groups, private research, and individual and group thinking—these are some of the procedures suggested for sessions.

Time, effort, and expense of preparing posters, chalkboards, and other learning aids will be more than amply repaid in attentiveness and retention of ideas studied.

The display poster illustrated here may be considered a bare minimum in learning aids. It is designed as the focal point for the entire study. A piece of signboard (28 x 44 inches) can be purchased at many paint stores. This is sturdy enough to stand without buckling. Cut the arrow from a small piece of bright-colored construction paper and glue it on an ordinary clothespin. Make the insert from poster paper and stand it on the easel at the bottom of the main poster.

Each time, move the pointer on the display poster to the chapter being studied.

The Message We Proclaim

Chapter:

1. Proclamation—The Christian Mission
2. Proclamation—A Biblical Theology
3. The Gospel We Proclaim—I
4. The Gospel We Proclaim—II
5. Proclamation Through Preaching
6. Proclamation Through Personal Witness
7. That by All Means We May Win Some
8. Dynamic for the Task

1. Proclamation and Me

Each of the eight inserts is planned to call attention to one of the most important topics in the chapter or to state the chapter topic. It is numbered to correspond to the chapter numbers:

1. Proclamation and Me
2. Preach or Teach?
3. What Should a Sermon Contain?
4. Salvation: God's Act; Man's Response
5. How Important Is Preaching?
6. Witness: Problems and Opportunities
7. Proclamation—in Many Ways
8. The Holy Spirit at Work

CHAPTER 1

Attach the pointer beside chapter one on the poster and put insert topic number one in place.

Create interest by the use of a chalkboard. (Poster paper or newsprint can be used if a chalkboard is not available.) Tell the class that you will give a word portrait; they are to identify the person. Write these descriptive words; *promoter, leader, administrator, financier, teacher, community leader, servant, prophet,* and *priest (preacher).*

Draw several rows of circles on the board. Write under the rows of circles: "What should happen?" Explain that the circles represent the congregation assembled for worship. Lead the members of the class to search the textbook for answers to the question.

Lecture briefly on "The Need to Understand Proclamation." Explain what is meant by proclamation.

Divide the class into four groups and assign to each group one of the "four theological demands for Christian proclamation" (section II). Ask each group to read and discuss its assignment for eight to ten minutes and to select one member of the group to give a summary of the discussion for the class.

Conclude with the summary given at the end of the chapter.

CHAPTER 2

Move the pointer to the theme for chapter 2 and place the second insert in position at the bottom.

Ask the participants to write on the inside cover of their books the heading "Sermon Content" and, below it, a number of subjects which should be treated in sermons. Ask several pupils to read their lists of topics. Invite comments as to why certain subjects should be included or not included. This will create a climate conducive to study of the material in this chapter.

On a chalkboard, write a number of key words and phrases. Write: "Proclaim means ____ ____." Invite definitions.

Discuss and illustrate from the Old Testament:

"Witness: within the covenant"

"Witness: beyond the covenant"

Describe the three areas of Christian witness foreseen in the Old Testament.

Guide members in learning the difference between "to herald," "to proclaim good news," and "to teach."

Help them to discover how the preaching of the apostles is distinguished from the preaching of Jesus.

Write these words on the chalkboard: *"kerygma"* and *"didache."* Define each word. State the author's viewpoint. Call attention to the insert "Preach or Teach?"

In closing, ask five members to read aloud the five important conclusions given at the end of the chapter.

CHAPTER 3

Ask the members to underscore in their textbooks the author's paraphrase of James S. Stewart at the beginning of this chapter. Call on several members to state in their own words what they understand the statement to mean. Lead the others to comment upon the author's statement "We are witnesses to a deed."

Word Search

Select several words which point up some of the main ideas in the chapter and write them on paper in letters large enough for everyone to see. Include these words: *task, deed, kerygma, Christ, gospel,* and *eternal life*. Direct a word search in the textbook.

Use the arrow to call attention to the display poster and add the insert for this chapter.

Film

Try to secure the film *Endued with Power* (18 min.; rental, black and white, $6.00; color, $9.00) for showing in this session. Divide the class into three listening teams. Assign to each team one of these areas of experience to watch and listen for: (1) evidences of the power of the Holy Spirit; (2) evidences of proclamation in Peter and John's healing of the beggar; (3) content of Peter's sermon at Pentecost.

Study Groups

Use this alternate plan if it is impossible to secure the film. Assign to each of three groups one of these topics: "The Preaching of Peter," "The Preaching of Stephen," and "The Preaching of Paul." After a ten-minute study period, call for a summary report from each group.

Conclusion

Close the study of this chapter by reading aloud the last two paragraphs of the chapter.

CHAPTER 4

Adjust the arrow pointer and the insert card.

Panel

In advance, enlist *nine* persons to serve on three panels. Assign to the three members of each panel one of the three divisions of this chapter for detailed study.

1. The Gospel—God's Act in Christ
2. The Gospel—What Christ Has Done for Man
3. Salvation—Past, Present, and Future

Each panel will be expected to discuss its topic before the class and then give the class members opportunities to ask questions and make comments.

Strip Chart

Interest in the three topics can be increased by the use of a strip chart. Write the topics on a chalkboard or poster and cover each one with a strip of paper. Pull each strip off when ready to discuss the topic hidden under it.

Study

Lead participants to consider this statement made by the author at the beginning of the chapter: "Basically, however, the apostles preached the *facts* of the gospel without comment or explanation. Interpretation of these facts occurs in the Gospels and Epistles." Ask whether these two statements seem to be valid in the light of our study in this session.

CHAPTER 5

Prior to this session, review the definitions of the word "primary." Display the word in some conspicuous manner as it is discussed.

Focus Attention

Direct the class to the chapter title and the topic as revealed by the arrow and insert on the display.

Mild Debate

Divide the class into two groups of equal size.

Introduce the first section of this chapter, "The Primacy of Preaching," in a manner that will provoke debate. Ask one group to take a *positive* position on each of the topics and the other group to take a *negative* position. For example, the positive group can give reasons why "Preaching is primary in the advance of Christianity." The negative group will cite reasons why "Preaching is not primary in the advance of Christianity."

State the topic clearly and encourage prompt, free exchange of thoughts from each group.

Section Summary

After each one of the three topics has been discussed thoroughly, give a brief summary from the textbook.

Lecture

Lecture on "Preaching as Redemptive History." Give emphasis under this heading to the following phrases: "the Word of God in three categories," "an audacious claim," "in preaching God acts," and "in the cross and resurrection the victory of God's purpose was achieved."

Sermon Objectives

Invite pupils to underscore the objectives of gospel sermons as given under "Preaching to Be Gospel Centered." Assign each one of the four objectives to a different person for a discussion of the meaning.

About Preaching

Write on the chalkboard "Revival in Preaching Depends upon." Ask the members to supply two words:

1. _____
2. _____

They may readily find the missing words in the textbook (*congregations* and *ministers*).

Conclusion

Comment on the author's statement that "Preaching costs."

CHAPTER 6

Adjust the arrow and the new insert in the usual manner.

Use Additional Reference

Well in advance of this session, assign to a pupil the section on "Verbal Witness" in *A Quest for Vitality in Religion* by Findley B. Edge (pp. 143-45). Ask him to summarize the main ideas.

Compare Translations

Bring to the class at least two modern-language translations of the New Testament. Have one person to read Ephesians 4:11-13 in the King James Version followed immediately by reading in the other translations. Invite comments on the passage.

Three Categories

Use material from the first section of the chapter and present the contemporary challenge of the church. This may be done in three categories: needs, obstacles, and obligations.

Brainstorming

Inform the members that the main objective in brainstorming is to get a large number of ideas out in the open. Interest will be best if participants can be inspired to respond as rapidly as possible. State the topic: "Personal *qualities* and *actions* which are necessary before Christians and churches can become effective as witnesses." Ask for immediate oral response. Have someone to make a written list as the qualities and actions are named. Review the list and mark those entries considered by the group to be of greatest value.

CHAPTER 7

After preparing the display poster for this session, review the entire list of chapter headings. Observe that through chapter 5 the study centered largely in preaching. In chapter 6, the emphasis began to shift, and now it becomes clear that proclamation includes many different and important kinds of experiences.

Study Groups

If there are sixteen or more in the class, divide the class into eight study groups. Assign to each group one of the eight topics in this chapter. Ask the groups to study for ten minutes and then give an oral digest of their findings.

If the eight topics are written on a chalkboard for everyone to see during the reports, more of the ideas can be retained.

Summary

State briefly the purpose of this chapter.

CHAPTER 8

Direct attention to the topics on the display posters.

This last chapter is marked by a deeply devotional quality. A study of the Holy Spirit is indeed a serious matter.

Begin by reading 1 Corinthians 2:3–5.

Lecture

Lecture briefly on each section of the chapter. Include many of the Scripture passages in reading aloud. These may be read by class members, preferably using two or three modern-language translations.